Get to Good

A Mantra for Life

JACQUELINE CORNABY

BALBOA
PRESS

A DIVISION OF HAY HOUSE

Balboa Press books may be ordered through booksellers or by contacting:

Balboa Press
A Division of Hay House
1663 Liberty Drive
Bloomington, IN 47403
www.balboapress.com
1-(877) 407-4847

ISBN: 978-1-4525-4111-2 (sc)
ISBN: 978-1-4525-4113-6 (hc)
ISBN: 978-1-4525-4112-9 (e)

Library of Congress Control Number: 2011918648

Because of the dynamic nature of the Internet, any web addresses or
links contained in this book may have changed since publication and
may no longer be valid. The views expressed in this work are solely those
of the author and do not necessarily reflect the views of the publisher,
and the publisher hereby disclaims any responsibility for them.

The author of this book does not dispense medical advice or prescribe the use
of any technique as a form of treatment for physical, emotional, or medical
problems without the advice of a physician, either directly or indirectly. The
intent of the author is only to offer information of a general nature to help
you in your quest for emotional and spiritual well-being. In the event you use
any of the information in this book for yourself, which is your constitutional
right, the author and the publisher assume no responsibility for your actions.

Any people depicted in stock imagery provided by Thinkstock are
models, and such images are being used for illustrative purposes only.
Certain stock imagery © Thinkstock.

Printed in the United States of America

Balboa Press rev. date: 11/29/2011

DEDICATIONS

I dedicate this book to God, My Hero Shayne and Princess Zara, My Family & Friends, and Clients who lovingly call me to be more. Your belief in me inspires me to become the Woman God intended me to be, Thank you for being You.

CONTENTS

ACKNOWLEDGMENTS

I would like to acknowledge the experience and enlightenment I am privileged to have received from Tony Robbins, Sai Baba and Abraham. Mostly, I acknowledge you for believing in your potential granting others permission to do the same. You are in the perfect place at the perfect time. All is Well!

Please accept this invitation to become a member of VIP Coaching

www.jacquelinecornaby.com

You are welcome to email me a thought, inquiry into Private Coaching and Speaking, or collaborative idea.

Jacqueline@jacquelinecornaby.com

Jacquelinecornaby@gmail.com

GET TO GOOD

Everything you want in your life comes with the thought that you will feel better in having it. Once you get it or get there then you can feel good. Why not take the shortcut to your desires and feel better now? By choice without contingencies permission granted *Get to Good!*

Your life is right now, it is not someday, when you get that promotion, new car, married or lose 10lbs. Many of you are looking for yourself and the good life in all the wrong places. You are one more shopping spree, anti-depressant, big money deal, elective surgery, and love affair away from truly finding yourself and enjoying the good life. Where is the Joie de Vivre? You think it is over there, they have it, over the next horizon, like chasing a shadow and you convince yourself why today is not the day to feel good but soon, after I make it happen, one day . . . perhaps. Pushing the pause button on life for the elusive dream, regret the past, worry about the future and distracted with the now . . . **Oh! My Stars** . . . one can see how this would leave you frustrated, powerless and disillusioned.

Take a breathe . . . now exhale . . . you are exactly where you intended to be and all is well. While postponing the good life may have been your modus operandi up until now, you do have choice in the matter and this book will show you the way. Whether you are a Mother who is trying to find balance and yourself . . . a professional trying to make a secure living and provide for your family, an entrepreneur or artist who wants to make it big, someone who is trying to find meaning to your life rather than feel stressed and depressed, a teenager trying to find your place in the world, or single and searching . . . the answers are closer and easier than you might think. Allow me to remind you of all that you are beyond behaviors you are the hero and heroine of your life. You may not feel that way right now, your behavior and life may be a reflection of the contrary but that is of no interest, our interest is upon amplifying your potential not your problems. You are the creator of your life experience and you are worthy of all of your desires. All is Well is your natural rhythm; whereas, pain and struggle were added by you after the fact through life experience, observing and justification. *Get to Good* will be your guide for the mantra **I am Worthy and All is Well** for accelerated abundance in all areas of your life.

What do you want for your life? Your response may be material items, career, relationship, health, financial freedom, peace of mind or all of the above. Think about it, there is not anything you desire that is for any other reason than you would feel better once realized. Consider the possibilities if you were able to condition yourself for feeling good in the moment anywhere anytime with anyone. All of this and more will be provided for you throughout the book. Is it really the desire that brings the better feeling or does the better feeling bring about the desire? Unlike the chicken and the egg dilemma where the jury is still out on which one came first, your thoughts and feelings supersede a realized outcome, invisible creates visible, whether you believe it or not; it is so. The intent is that by the time you finish the book you will not only believe it but you will begin to implement it into your own life. Introducing *Get to Good A Mantra for Life* for feeling good now and being a match to your desires. ***All desires come from alignment.***

I acknowledge you for all that you are and look forward to who you will become. This book was written with you in mind, offering you how to think rather than what to think. Beyond memorization or just more knowledge, *how to think* allows you to recall at will. You have all you need within you, allow this book to be a reminder, you are in the perfect place and time, nothing is wrong or needs fixing for a transformation to exist. Thank you for being you. It becomes you!

Being a spokesperson for empowerment, I have the privilege to coach private individuals and speak publicly worldwide which allows me to continue my curiosity and insight into human potential. The intent is to bring my experience to you in the introduction of a book. My clients range from CEO's, Entrepreneurs, Professionals, Homemakers, and Students to those who are seeking who they want to be when they grow up. One thing they all share in common just like you is belief in the potential of the human spirit.

The intention behind *Get to Good* is to allow your potential to come out and play! ***Permission Granted!*** You are going to read it, hear it, say, think and see it abundantly so it becomes A Mantra for Life: *Get to Good!*

Allow me to set the stage for integrating *Get to Good* as a lifestyle for you. As you read, profound knowledge will be offered for paradigm shifts in thinking for you to access your potential anywhere, anytime with anyone. Think of *Get to Good* Lifestyle as an effortless way of being and enjoying the life you are creating.

Throughout the book you will notice **mantras in bold**, practice using them in your daily life as A Mantra for Life. Notice I said practice not perfect. Utilize only the mantras that resonate for you. At the end of the book and weaved throughout, *Get to Good* Lifestyle Conditioning is included for further integration of the insights and knowledge. For you overachievers and analyzers patience grasshopper, give yourself the opportunity for shifts in thinking before understanding how to implement otherwise it will be a superficial fix. As you evolve you will want to reread the book for new meaning and integration as it relates to you. Shall we begin?

Do you ever wonder why some days are better than others? You wake up and wonder why did I get out of bed this morning? Think having the good life is really coincidence, luck, and favoritism? If so, you can see how this would leave you feeling powerless and chaotic, the good news is the good life is linked back to you. You look at your bank account and wonder why you do not have more money or when will your ship come in? You look at your relationships and wonder when will he show up or when will she leave? You have desires but most of you think your desires are contingent upon something or someone outside of you. Contingency desires are limiting and never a true reflection of your potential. **Potential transcends logic.** Your current state of affairs does not have to be your consistent reality. What is real? That which you give your attention combined with evidence to support your reality.

If you wait until the evidence of what you want shows up before you feel better than you will be left with more waiting. Most people have the sequential order reversed for realizing their desires with an attitude of "let me see it then I will believe it." What if you were able to access feeling good before the evidence of your desire showed up? You would be a match to your desires and by universal law the evidence would show up in your experience and by the way sooner than later. Empower your life. *Empowerment is the power to control your world.*

So here it goes: If you cannot *Get to Good* then you cannot get the Good Life! *Get to Good* is a mindset for alignment with the good life, the one worthy of you! The answers you are seeking come from being aligned as an empowered person.

I hear your voices declaring, "Wait a minute, it cannot be that easy, I have to work hard, struggle, shed my share of sweat and tears, earn my way to the winners' circle and then maybe just maybe I can have it all, or at least more than I have now. I simply cannot just sit back and pretend everything is going to be fine because it is not. I have bills to pay, a family to provide for, a boss to answer to, and the reality of life." Listen, I am not condoning inaction or wearing rose colored glasses, what I am certain about is you are the creator of your world, *as you think it and feel it you create it.* If you choose stress as your modus operandi then you perpetuate more stress in your life and confuse it as reality, it does not have to be so for you. Knowing my audience, you of all people have the power to rise above stress and your current reality and see your world from a new perspective. As a society we have resigned to being stressed about today and worried about the future. The only time stress enters your world is when you are not in the moment, many times you are either worrying about the future or wishing you could change the past. ***Stress is a buzzword for fear and worry is the misuse of your mind.*** Enlighten me, when has worry ever been productive for you? Exactly. Borrowing from worry is synonymous to a loan shark; nothing good can come from it. Who needs enemies when you have a mind full of worried thoughts? So you continue the perpetual cycle of exchanging this moment for the next in hopes that it will get better, it just has to get better, but it will never get better until you *Get to Good.*

Intentional Moments

Why is it that some of you think if you can just bypass this moment and the next few thousand or million that you will get to your arrival place quicker and be pleased with the destination? We are a very results driven world, point A to point B, giving more satisfaction to checking off the "To Do List" than experiencing the being and doing while getting it done. You look at your day or week and wonder how am I going to get it all done? But your outcome for life is not to get it all done. The purpose of life is to appreciate who you are today with anticipation for tomorrow. Rather most of you are waiting until you can exclaim *"TGIF"* for the weekend to get here so you can breathe, relax and enjoy. What about Monday through Thursday do those days not matter in the life of you? ***News Flash:*** This is your life why would you wish it away? What if you lived fully on a Monday allowing you to expand your desires for Tuesday? Up until now, many of you have been focused upon making it happen, where you push and figure it all out, intellectualize it never mind your feelings and thoughts what do they have to do with it anyway? This way of living is never ending like the mail it just keeps coming and coming so too will more items on your to do list. And more stress on your mind. Why do you think the term *going postal,* no disrespect to postal workers, is referred to as perpetual frustration? What happens when you do check off all the items on your To Do List, then what? Is it all over or do you become a professional list maker rather than pure potential ever expanding? ***Interesting. A Hint: On purpose will transcend a "to do" list every time.***

I know why you think and do it this way, believe me I have done it more times than I care to remember, I simply want you to know it does not have to be the way for you anymore. You are not your behavior. Consider some more paradigm shifts in thinking so you can be compelled to *Get to Good.* For instance, escaping this moment because you think you need to get on to the next big thing or simply just get through the day is called existing. In every moment you are either expanding or existing. All future experiences are caused by the way you embrace or avoid the moments. Escaping the moment is prevalent in those who have never really experienced the joy and infinite potential in the moment. While never truly being satisfied with this moment, experiencing a few fleeting magical moments and you can begin to think this is the way it is for me this is My Life. Dodge this moment for the next; trade this one for the next best thing, what is behind curtain number one, looking for the shortcut only to come up short. Too afraid to feel all the emotions life is willing to offer you in this moment you skip to fast forward or rewind your life searching and hoping something or someone will fulfill you. Practicing insanity and thinking one day, as soon as, if only, all the reasons why now is not the right time to be present to life which by the way is the only place your dreams reside. Life is not waiting out a storm; it is learning how to dance in the rain. You have a list of reasons why you should not or cannot but you only need one reason why you can today. The secret behind this is you are the only one who can cause you to act on behalf of you without compromise. *You are the creator of your world.*

So why would you put off today? Many of you go into distraction and avoidance for fear of the unknown. You begin to imagine all the ways your life may or may not unfold; it can be long term or even the unknown about this week, tomorrow or later today. It may be about spending this moment thinking only about what is to come: the next meeting, business call, lunch, this evening, children's schedule, or the weekend. And if you think once the event is here you will be present to it you are mistaken for the same habitual thinking will continue to occur unless you are willing to shift your thoughts to now. Reliving the past or wondering about the future does not allow space for life in the present, the here and now, the moments that will create the pathway toward the future. The only way to get to the future is to live in the now. What is the big hurry to get to the future, it will get here and the past is complete. Reminisce on the past and visualize the future, just do not stare or stay too long in either tense, so you can continue to create intentional moments.

In every moment you have a choice Love or Fear. Your thoughts, feelings, actions, and behaviors reside in one of these two categories Good and Not So Good. Love would be all that serves you and others while fear would be all that destroys you and others. Love contributes; fear contaminates. One aspect of fear is worry, many people worry and they never equate it to fear or negative thinking rather they back up their worry with justification, logic, sophisticated excuses and more. Worry and its relative's anxiety, self-doubt and insecurity can have your life in a perpetual negative spin. Intellectualizing your fear only creates more fear. Worry has you neither here nor there leaving you powerless to control and create your world.

At the other end of the spectrum, chaos can occur when you do not see far enough beyond current circumstance, when thinking an event is global and means everything. For example, if your partner forgets to bring home a bottle of wine as requested you make it mean that he does not love you or you receive an unexpected bill in the mail and you make it mean you can never get ahead or a business meeting goes awry you make it mean you may not be cut out for this line of work or life goes manic you think what is it all about anyway? When you lose sight of possibilities your world becomes final and finite. Or when you tend to think as soon as I accomplish this or complete this or achieve this or have this then my life can begin, then I will have all the time in the world to meditate, take leisurely walks, sip on my latte, get my body in shape, have time for a partner, start a family, build my empire and finally be present. As soon as the children are grown, my husband and I will have private time together or as soon as the holidays are over then I will begin my nutrition and exercise program.

All this to say, "It would be nice but not now for I have this thing figured out, let me finish all of this and then I can exhale and give my life the attention it deserves." All the while your dreams become intellectualized to death. For now what you are really saying is my life does not matter for I am not that interested in living into my full potential and being present to the abundant moment available to me now. So I will begin when my life is over, when I ascend from this plane, is this life of yours just to pass time, in the meantime or is it an opportunity to magnify your pure potential each and every moment? Who said today had to be one big action list as a means to an end, just passing through, was it you that agreed to these terms and conditions? Perhaps it is time to rethink your agreement. And for some of you it may not be quite this dramatic, *Get to Good* may be a powerful reminder of appreciating the person you are today complemented with anticipation for what is to come. *Give attention only to that which is worthy of you.*

I can appreciate there is always something you can fill your time up with but does it expand and reflect your potential? Distraction is the infamous dream stealer. There is a dream inside everyone of us, how long will it be stored inside of you before you begin living it out moment by moment? An empowered moment affects your world now and in the future. It is where the best of you can be found, known as alignment, if you will allow it. *This moment will be as good as you allow it to be.* When you choose to *Get to Good* in the moment you set the tone for the next moment of allowing good to come into your experience. Your life is made up of moments, if you want to see your future look to the present moment; it trumps a fortuneteller or crystal ball every time. To live within integrity or alignment of the moment is to live with intention. A paradigm shift in the definition of *integrity being what I want is how I feel*. *Get to Good Lifestyle Conditioning: Begin to feel good about your future desires now.*

Life is not just about what did I do today but who was I and how did I feel today? While if you simply chose to *Get to Good* you would set your mind in motion toward what you want and allow inspired action to follow as you realized your desires. Your desires have nothing to do with your action. Your desires have to do with your thoughts and feelings. When you are feeling good you are inspired to move in the direction of your dreams, life becomes effortless and joyful; your desires become manifested and continue to expand. Think of a time in your life when you honored your body with exercise or movement more than likely the endorphins from exercise inspired you to take better nutritional decisions even for a moment and a willingness to do good for your body. This mindset not only affected your health but I would imagine positively influenced other areas of your life from relationships to career. What if you allowed the momentum of good to perpetuate in your life, imagine the possibilities. This is intentional living. *It becomes you.*

Sophisticated Excuses

The only reason you choose not to *Get to Good* is sophisticated excuses. Beyond what used to be called excuses people have now moved to sophisticated excuses because they can get away with retelling them and having buy in from family and friends, colleagues and online chat groups relating on their sophisticated excuses. These are justifications, reasons, excuses, small stories, and logic disguised as sophisticated, acceptable excuses as to why you cannot have your desires or have them *yet*. Their only flaw is they postpone your life, your desires and your potential. *A Hint:* I am being a bit mischievous, sophisticated excuses are a huge oversight.

Here is a glimpse into the look of sophisticated excuses: too busy right now to think, do not have the bandwidth, not enough money, time or energy, as soon as . . . until he then I can . . . if only . . . one day, so long as . . . . Sophisticated excuses all originate from lack mentality combined with internal and external contingencies. My Spouse, my children, my childhood, the government, my boss, my career, the economy, my body, my schedule, my bank account, my education . . . all limiting beliefs that keep you telling a sophisticated excuse again and again of why you cannot at least not yet. When you use your partner, child, employee, truly anyone or anything as your reason for not being aligned with *Get to Good* it is a sophisticated excuse. If you use your partner as a reason for not feeling loved and adored, your boss for not feeling fulfilled and prosperous with your career, your child for not feeling like a good parent or the world for not living your purpose, well then you are giving attention to all that is powerless and false in your world rather than the empowered you. *What if everyone you knew was off the hook of your empowerment?*

Not to mention indulgent excuses: the need to be right, a people pleaser, self-compromising and denial of worth lend themselves to sophisticated excuses. *There is nothing right about feeling bad.*

Stress is a sophisticated excuse; while widely accepted among society, it is simply fear in disguise. So when you tell yourself or another you are stressed what you are really saying is I am in fear, I am fearful. Speaking powerfully commands a greater level of self respect. Do you think if you no longer hid behind your sophisticated excuses you would no longer be disillusioned by the stipulations that must happen before you have your desires? You would speak powerfully to others and yourself, a call to be more than a savvy storyteller. As a bonus, precious time would open up on your agenda for the good life when you do not waste the moments on sophisticated excuses.

It is important that you know, at times you are simply not going to want to *Get to Good!* Believe me I know this first hand, my halo slips daily and it is unbecoming. I have traded my halo for horns countless times and my husband has informed me he now knows what the devil looks like without question. I spin it and call it role playing; I thought men love an alter ego, now

I know differently. So I breathe, say a mantra and *Get to Good.*
A Hint: The formula for creating The Good Life.

Your ego will want to keep you stuck thinking small. The only
role of the ego is to protect itself not you. So in these moments
when sophisticated excuses are heightened *Get to Good* Anyway!
Get to Good Lifestyle Conditioning will guide you in accessing
good anywhere anytime with anyone in the moment. Getting
to know good as it relates to you is priceless and powerful.

Pause for a moment and read this: Nothing good can come
from a sophisticated excuse no matter how justified you are, in
the end, it is you who denies yourself the desires, placing them
in a holding pattern outside of your experience. When you
truly get just how powerful you are you will come to realize
that you are the creator of your world, everyone and everything
is off the hook of your having The Good Life. What a relief!
Now you can simply enjoy creating, imagining and expanding
from where you are today, it is the ideal starting place for you.
You have the power to place yourself as the Hero or Heroine
in the story of your life rather than the victim or martyr.

Said another way and worth reiterating, even if you do not feel
like it *Get to Good!* Try it on, embrace it, celebrate noticing
when you feel less than good rather than beating yourself up or
fixating upon it, you may have been doing not so good for long
enough, no coincidence you are reading this book; this is your
time! Welcome to The Good Life! The power lies within you.
Please accept this invitation to remind you of your potential
and live by the mantra *Get to Good!*

Well, I would like to but if you only knew my circumstance
then you would understand why I feel this way. ***News Flash:***

attention all readers, so you are clear, I am going to relate on all that you are rather than all that you are not; a concentrated intention upon magnifying your potential not your problems. Listen, any of us could amplify our problems and feel bad in a hurry. Let us not relate on the small stories, my promise to you is to speak to your potential, this is time well spent anything less is *nonsense*. **You are more than your circumstance.**

While your circumstance may be less than desirable perhaps it is time to transcend reality with a better feeling thought and feeling? You cannot continue to talk about and relive the complaint and not eventually join in the party. You may have debt but continuing to talk about the debt only perpetuates more of the same. Debt, bills and collectors all appear real but you will want to give more of your attention to your desires of what you want rather than the reality of what is. Talk about the solution, what you want, and the new desired story. RSVP: No Thank you, to a pity party. I want to go to a Good Party! Of course! Your life becomes that which you focus upon, even if you think you are justified in your complaint because they are wrong and you are right, eventually you become party to the complaint as well. It would be like jumping in a swimming pool and think you are not going to get wet, a smidge delusional. Will you make it about someone luring you in the water, being pushed in or perplexed as to how you became soaked? *Get to Good Lifestyle Conditioning: Breathe, say a mantra and Get to Good.*

Narrated by You

If you want to shift your future you will want to shift your now. If you continue to tell the story of *what is* then you cannot give your attention to *what you want*. You cannot keep measuring, regurgitating, and convincing yourself and others about what is and expect to get what you want. You will never be a match to your desires; you will only be a match to the current circumstance. For when you tell it like it is and if like it is happens to be less than desirable then you only perpetuate more of *what is*. It is similar to practicing insanity, doing the same thing over and over again and expecting a different result. Even if what is appears real, logical and justifiable; it is all the same, hiding behind the mask of sophisticated excuses. And when you continue to tell it like it is you are telling the future as well. Transcend reality with concentrated attention upon what you want. Create a new reality with your thoughts of today and vision for the future. Talk about your desires and begin to look for good in your day today. Implement a *Get to Good lifestyle conditioning question: What do I want? Look for what you want today.* Now for those of you who like what is then yes continue to tell what is and expand from that platform. This is the intention for all to get to the place where you feel good about what is and excited for what is to come.

Perhaps it is time for you to tell a new story one that is worthy of you. A new level of thinking is founded upon the belief that you think on a higher level today than you did yesterday. There is what is so and there is creation; think beyond what is so. If you are willing to think bigger than you get all the rewards that come from The Good Life. The same level of thinking that brought you to today will not get you to tomorrow. *A Call to Be More.* No, not everyone is doing it but you can and why not? The Universe will play with you on the level of your thinking. Co-creating with the Universe will be aligned with the ability to think beyond what is so. I call small thinking micro thinking and it is not worthy of your time. Elevate your mind and you elevate your life experience, this is where your talent is best utilized. Allow your thoughts to be of high frequency. High frequency thoughts are empowered with intention upon who you are, what it is you want and feeling good about your desires now.

You live in an all inclusive Universe, whatever you give your attention to will be included in your experience, be mindful of what you are including in your thinking and your story telling. Mindful rather than monitor so you can be in tune, shift in the moment and *Get to Good!*

Telling a success story, a love story or a triumphant story offers you an opportunity to conspire with the Universe complemented by your Faith, to put your intentions in motion expecting desires to manifest. Being in concert with The Laws of the Universe allows for effortless prosperity. Align yourself with good feeling thoughts for being a match to the life you really want. *Get to Good Lifestyle Conditioning Questions: How can I be a match to my desires? What will I conjure up today? Who will I collaborate with today?*

Take a moment to reflect on the story of your life: Your emotional state, your bank account, your physical body, your relationships . . . want more, wondering why you are not where you thought you would be, not as happy as you hoped, finances could use a few more commas and zeros at the end than debt, not quite the physique you would like for yourself, still looking for Mr. Right or simply co-existing in your marriage? The good news is it is up to you and perhaps at times the not so good news is it is up to you, no blame game only empowerment. You have all the power to create it the way you want it, to be the cause in your life for you are the creator of your thoughts and your effect on life. So many of you want to blame the outside world, circumstances, time, money, the boss, the cat, partner or spouse, the devil, but in the end all ownership ultimately belongs to one person whom you know intimately . . . you. While the alternative may provide relief it is merely superficial. Many times you give your power away to someone else and they are so busy checking out their own reflection in the mirror they do not have a clue that you too are expecting them to deliver. To be causative in your life allows you to claim your power back; otherwise, you give all of your energy and power to sophisticated excuses, stories and others about why you have not achieved the optimal result. Do you really want to tell that story again? *You are worthy of your desires.*

A story written with small thinking is an excuse in disguise, a sophisticated excuse, it is the reasoning and justification you have been telling yourself and others about why you do not have what it is you want and So It Is! You spin the story of your life hoping your sophisticated excuse will not be exposed while retelling it until one day you actually believe it is real. The only reason you do not have all that you want is the story about why you cannot have it or cannot have it yet. *Yet* being the very word that has you stall and postpone your life for one day in the future but certainly not today with this being the same story years from now unless you change your story.

A story if told by small thinking will have you stall on your desires if told by big thinking will have you accelerate your dreams. We hear people say "Oh that is the story of my life," "What is his story?" And how often do you tell your story over and over again, whether it is your internal self talk or to everyone you know and even those you do not know, truly you tell it to anyone who will listen. You let it play out in your internal dialogue all day long subconsciously, until you actually believe it. And although it may sound and appear logical, is it really true or a skewed perception? *The Buddha taught that pain arises out of ignorance by which he meant not a lack of knowledge, but rather a misperception of reality.*

Perhaps your story is outdated, you recorded the story years ago on a cassette player or even an 8 track tape for those of you who can remember and now we are in the age of MP3 players, bypass CD's what is next? But you are still committed to playing your story one more time on a warped tape or scratched disc because it is what you know and there is something to be said for certainty. Certainty at least gives us the same result time and time again, but is it the optimal result, a reflection of your highest self? What is the soundtrack playing in your head? Does it serve you?

You must be willing to stretch yourself, elevate your mind, and think bigger if you are to create a new story for your life. To be the cause in your life states you are the one to take ownership for your life, until you embrace this moment with ownership life becomes a perpetual delusion. Ownership needs few words . . . I AM, I Do, I Will, I Love You, I Apologize, Thank You, My Pleasure; anything else weakens your position for being grounded in your intention. While some of you who have stood at the marriage alter would have liked the opportunity to offer a run on sentence to *I Do so long as* . . . it would be better scripted for a romantic comedy or soap opera than a love affair. An empowered voice does not need filler, a run on sentence, baggage or justification, it is where no story is needed, allowing you to let go of the small story and speak from a place of empowerment narrated by your highest self.

For those of you who say I am willing to take ownership but what about the role of Karma, well then yes what about Karma? Many view Karma as a negative, out of your control, chance or predestined but Karma simply means Action. So if you want to create what you might perceive as good Karma in your life take action in a positive way. Allow your actions to be a reflection of your highest self. Intentional *Get to Good* action produces harmony or reaction produces chaos.

Dear Get to Good Reader, my invitation to you is to take inspired action from a place of alignment so that it serves you and others and together we will produce desirable effects. You are worthy to be the cause in your life and it is time you realized this truth. Love, Karma

You live within the parameter of your stories. The star character is you and you are either placing yourself as the Hero or Heroine or the Villain or Victim. The success stories tell of a time you triumphed, achieved, and prevailed, the small stories tell of an elaborate reason why you did not make it happen, rather than gaining the wisdom from the lesson, many of you become in a trance state. So it is your story that supports or interferes with your causative actions in producing desirable effects known as The Good Life defined by you.

Think about anything you want in your life and why you still do not have it manifested . . . happiness, love, peace, money, joy, fulfilling relationships, health and fitness, rewarding career . . . what is your story? Does it serve you? Does it bring you closer to your dreams or keep you out of reach? Compel or repel? Are you more committed to your current position or story or could you be open to being committed to a story narrated by your Higher Self? A Story told by an aligned you will find itself as a best seller as a success story, a love affair, happily ever after . . . perhaps it is time to rewrite the story of your life, a bigger story that is aligned with your integrity and identity. One where your story is a reflection of your worthiness. Small story small life, big story big life! Rather than tell it like it is begin to tell it how you want it and anticipate something great is about to happen.

Shortcut to Desires

Allow me to mind read, do you have reason to postpone *Get to Good*, perhaps? Please know that if you choose this now you are choosing ignorance . . . the choice to ignore your potential and give attention to your problem. *Magnify your potential not your problems.* The choice will always be yours. Intelligence is that now you know you have choice in the matter, in the moment, what have you got to lose? For starters, letting go of stress, sophisticated excuses, and resistance to all that is good. What have you got to gain? Accessing feeling good while manifesting the life you desire. Simply put: *Get to Good!* Be mindful that living by the mantra *Get to Good* may not always make sense in the moment but go there anyway. We move on emotion and justify with logic. It matters not how you *Get to Good* so long as you allow it more often than not. *Alignment transcends reality.*

Here is a priceless whisper: Nothing more needs to happen for you to *Get to Good!* It is not reserved for the few it is available to you in your life right now, you are a member of A VIP Club. There is nothing enlightened about denying your potential for *empowerment is a natural resource.* Permission Granted by you! Exhale . . . Allow yourself to come out and play as the person you were intended to be without the disguise of sophisticated excuses. Many of you have become Pros at feeling stress and chaos, now it is time to get to know you and how it is to feel good. Be free for **liberation is a state of mind not a destination.**

If everything you want is for the reason that you will feel better in having it, then why not access feeling good now? The Law of Attraction says *Like attracts Like.* If what you want feels good then would it not make sense to be the one feeling good so as to attract good? I feel good therefore I attract good. And the more I continue to attract the better I feel allowing more good to flow into my experience. I am the creator of my good life! **As I influence my thought I influence my life.** *I Love It!*

Notice none of this is contingent upon a time frame, circumstance (people, place, thing, event or experience) or who you have been up until now. It is a choice *Get to Good* or not! The sooner the better it gets. I want that over there, once I get there then I will feel better, my life will be good. For now, I will postpone feeling good for I do not have evidence of the good life yet. **Hint:** Sophisticated excuse in disguise. Wanting more is a good thing, wanting more because right here where you are today and right now is not enough will only produce more lack.

Think of something you desire. What is the feeling you have associated to having the desire manifested? For instance, if you desire prosperity, more money, and financial success, what is the feeling you have associated with having more money? Certainty, pride, accomplishment, excitement, relief, freedom . . . what is your feeling? Access that feeling now. If you can access the feeling that is attributed to the desire you want *before* the desire is manifested you have discovered the true power of creation.

Transforming the invisible into visible is available to you. On the contrary, if you wait until the evidence of your desire shows up before you begin to access the feeling associated with your desire . . . you will be left waiting. If you want more money over there but you feel bad right now you will not be a match to money. I need more money is noticing the absence of money rather than accessing the feeling of already having more than enough money. Remember to access the feelings associated to *what you want* rather than *what is* and you will be a match.

The feelings or essence associated with your desires are circulating in your life right now, go ahead and claim them today. Begin to feel them in your body, allow your thoughts to reflect good and look for evidence of those desired feelings in your day. You move within the expectation of your desires; expect for good to show up in your life. If thoughts become things, then your greatest work is to think good thoughts now. Said another way; my greatest work is to feel good now. Perhaps a paradigm shift in what *work* looks like for you will be helpful. The majority of your work that will produce a favorable result has nothing to do with action but rather your emotional state. Action outside of alignment is misplaced action. Now when you grant yourself permission to feel good today you become aligned and a match to your desires and by law desires will come into your experience. The action part will be you inspired and on purpose to take decisions in the moment. **Permission granted** by you.

It is important to realize that this is not a magic act, voodoo or wonder pill; the power of your thought is working for you right now, if you are having a less than good day allow us to go back to the thoughts you were thinking and the feelings you were emitting and with certainty they would be a match to less than good. It can work in your favor as well evidence of a good day is brought about by good thoughts and good feelings. Now you get the opportunity to conspire with The Universal Law rather than feel like it is an anomaly. Remember you are the fortuneteller for what is to come by the thoughts you think and emotions you feel in this moment. You are either allowing abundance to flow into your experience or you are not. There is not bad flowing in the Universe; it is simply a case of you not allowing the good to flow toward you; permission or denial by you. The Universe is responding to your consistent thoughts not haphazard offerings. *Amplify your desires.* Feel fortunate to be you!

The intention for *Get to Good* is not the absence of contrasting moments rather that you are either unaffected or you sharpen your desires and preferences when contrast is present. Invincible feelings governed by you, a love of life rather than a fear of failing, playing to win vs. playing not to lose, dialed in to your feelings rather than numbing or avoiding them, and empowered rather than powerless.

You do understand that you are doing the thinking anyway, does your thinking serve you? You are feeling someway right now; does your emotional state serve you? Is it a match to your desires or sophisticated excuses? Choose Wisely. It is your natural state to feel good; it is exhausting to pretend to be justified in feeling anything but good. Go ahead and exhale . . .

Power is found in redirecting your thoughts and feelings toward your desires beyond sophisticated excuses. It is so much easier to say *Yes* to you and your desires then retell, rewrite or spin a sophisticated excuse. *Less is More.*

Good and Not So Good

The quality of good is not limited to only good or considered to be less than excellent, impeccable, extraordinary or best. It is to be thought of in two categories, Good and Not So Good. There is only a source of good; if you are not allowing good it may translate into your experience as less than good. To be clear there is not a source of bad or less than good flowing in the world; you are the creator of your experience by allowing or resisting good. Transcend the thought of Good and Evil, Ying and Yang, or Highs and Lows. Think of good as anything that feels good. If your answer to the question *Do I feel good? Is* yes then it falls under Good. If on the other hand, your answer is anything but yes than it falls under Not So Good. Clarity is power, it is a Yes or No answer only; anything more would be a sophisticated excuse. The range on the emotional scale is relative to you in relation to your desires. Move with the emotion that feels better authentically, all are interlinked rather than a linear scale, only you can know the meaning behind the emotion, and you will continue to promote better feelings as you ease into the emotional scale.

If you decided today that you were going to look for evidence of good, beginning with you, you would find it. ***You live into your expectations.*** Be mindful of one thing that is good and allow it to show itself to you and grow exponentially.

To feel good simply for the sake of feeling good, no strings attached, will afford you the experience of The Good Life as scripted by you.

Snapshot of Good and Not So Good

Good

Not So Good

Good	Not So Good
Love	Fearful
Worthy	Unworthy
Aligned	Insecure
Abundant	Worried
Empowered	Stressed
Passionate	Angry
Purposeful	Justified
Joyful	Disappointment
Happy	Debilitated
Excited	Powerless
Inspired	Irritated
Liberated	Frustrated
Powerful	Overwhelmed
Creative	Pessimistic
Adored	Resentful
Energetic	Doubtful
Clarity	Indecisive
Compelled	Exhausted
Intentional	Sad
Magnetic	Depressed
Peaceful	Lonely
Bliss	Lost
Youthful	Distracted
Playful	Hopeless
Centered	Paranoid
Grounded	Anxious
Present	Controlling

Mantra

The Word Mantra translates to Ma=Mind Tra=Protector. What have you been filling your mind up with lately? How would you describe the private dialogue taking place between you and you, empowering or disempowering? The power of thought allows you to redirect your thinking so that it serves you for you get whatever you focus upon. *Science tells us two things cannot occupy one space at the same time.* So if your mind is filled with thoughts that serve you then limiting thoughts cannot be present. The same holds true if you fill your mind with disempowering thoughts you cannot have room for abundance. I get whatever I think about whether I want it or not; what do I want?

My mantra is my invitation. What and who have you been inviting into your experience with your thoughts? What are you being intentional about in your life? What are you planning? All is well or all is hell? Your external world is a reflection of your internal world. If you like what you see on the outside continue thinking and feeling good if not *Get to Good!* What are you waiting for? Your life is right now it is not someday or as soon as . . . remember life is made up of moments. This moment causes the next, what are you creating for your future with your thoughts and feelings of today? Does it serve you? Yes you have plenty of reasons why you cannot; however, we want to relate only on that which serves you. A *Get to Good lifestyle conditioning question for you to ask all day in all areas of your life: Does this serve me?* It will shift your thinking and feeling to all that is good and redirect you toward your desires, compelling rather than repelling. It is the intentional moments not the minutes that matter. And you matter!

If the only thing you lived by were *Get to Good* moments, think nano shifts, you would create the life you desire that becomes you. Living by the mantra *Get to Good* and you could close the book and enjoy the good life; however, please continue reading it too will be worthwhile. *Get to Good* is your invitation to come out and play as the man or woman God intended. **Oh My Stars It Becomes You!**

Be mindful and celebrate you now noticing when you do not feel good and being willing to *Get to Good*. Remember before reading this book you may have taken *what is* as face value now you are reminded of the power you have in every moment. The mantra *Get to Good* signals your subconscious that you acknowledge having infinite potential and you can access it at will. Priceless is the person who can call upon potential in the moment. Contrast of what you do not want is an opportunity for you to fine tune your desires. Get off it and *Get to Good*.

To give attention to only that which is worthy of you! *The mind does not know the difference between real or imagined.* Use your imagination to serve you. Life will be as good as you allow it to be.

A Mantra is a conditioned thought! Condition in the mantra *Get to Good* and allow it to become a way of life for you, Begin Now!

IT IS ALL GOOD

It is all good proposes the thought of abundance. Abundance beyond prosperity, including but not limited by financial only, abundance is an all inclusive mentality. An abundant mentality speaks of *All that I am, All that I want, All that I desire, All that I have, All that is good and All that is right*. It presupposes you are worthy, and you are, and then all thinking can come from this space. Whatever you are giving attention to in your life you are including in your thought process; does it serve you? (Voila, *Get to Good* lifestyle conditioning question, no coincidence I want it to be top of the mind for you.)

Lack mentality would then be an all exclusion mentality, primary exclusion being worthiness. Lack mentality takes the stance of denying one's greatness with *All that I am not, All that I do not want, All that I do not desire, All that I do not have or have yet, All that is less than good and All that is wrong*. The only thing lack mentality includes is a sophisticated excuse to remain more committed to lack than shifting toward abundance.

What is on your mind, the dialogue between you and you? For whatever you focus on you create, do you like what you have created, want more, want to get rid of that which you do not like, allow *Get to Good* to show you how to think and you decide what to think. You are always creating either positive or negative if you will. Every thought offers either the absence or presence of desire. Where do you spend the majority of your energy and focus on all that you want in life or all that you do not want? Most people will let you know right up front all that they do not want or do not like; while it might be helpful to a degree, if you stay here too long it will never give you what you want. Ask a woman what she wants in a man and more times than not she will tell you everything she does not want in a man referencing her recent heartache as a benchmark. If this is a client of mine then this is the time I use my southern charm and with a smile and direct eye contact I say, "That simply was not the question, that would have been the answer to the question what or who will you no longer tolerate in your life? I asked what do you want"? Or you might be saying I want more money but instead you are thinking and talking about the absence of money in your life.

You cannot continue to look at what is and get what you want. You cannot look at unwanted and get wanted. If you give attention and intention to focusing on what you do want and all that is good you can expect to create more of it again and again. A proven success formula. What percentage of your thought is abundant?

Do you think there is never enough or plenty to go around when it comes to time, space, material possessions, success, big deals, soul mates, ideas, and money? Do you find yourself saying I do not have the time, I am too busy, I cannot afford that right now, jealous or critical of others who have a lot, when is it my turn and why me? Longing for more things in your life only to find you are too busy to enjoy them once you have them or complain and question when your desires show up never mind simply saying *Thank You.* Are you chasing the illusion of desires never to be caught?

The polarity of thinking ranges from abundance to scarcity. Abundance is infinite, seeing your world through the eyes of eternity, it is creative, present and possibility thinking. It is where you know the potential for who you are and your life as being eternal and expansive. Scarcity is finite, limited and never enough; its premise is lack, all that I am not and all that I do not have in this life. The notion of not enough time or money, not enough of me represents thought formulating into negative or lack manifestation. Scarcity is worrying about the future and holding on to the setbacks of the past. More than its measurable qualities, scarcity skewed thinking is warped with the illusion that if others have something or someone you want then that means less for you. Envy, jealousy and competition are all traits of scarcity. Comparison and control is covert for insecurity. *It is interesting to me that people waste energy spending time envying others whom they would never wish to be.* Ponder that for a moment. Abundance thinking feeds off the mentality "Like Attracts Like" so one welcomes others to succeed and prefers to be around those who live in abundant mentality for they know the energy of co-creation. This is where you want to spend your time collaborating and contributing with other thought leaders; it expands your mind and dreams, always a good thing for you and the greater good. Truly there is nothing enlightened about being a big fish in a small pond or condemning the big fish in the big pond. Call upon your abundant nature.

A lack mindset cannot produce abundance. Focusing on all that you do not have and do not want rather than all you have and want is a lack mindset. To want what you already have is positive creation or abundance. To want for nothing is bliss. You always get what you really want and what you really do not want. Whatever you focus upon you will get, where do you spend the majority of your thinking and energy? Is it on all that you want or all that you do not want, all that is right or all that is wrong, all that you are or all that you are not? Positive or negative consequence begins with your thinking. If you are not intentional with your thinking you will resort to default thinking, which can be destructive in your positive creating and lead to less than desirable manifestations.

How you perceive time can be directly related to your level of joy directed by an abundant or scarce mindset. *Einstein said, "Time is just an illusion."* If you are always in a hurry, always running late or feel there is not enough time in the day then you will be stressed all the time and produce more lack based circumstances. Always being subject to the clock, calendar and sunlight has one feel like a prisoner to what is next without giving attention to what is now. More time is spent worrying about what happened or what may happen than what is happening in this moment. I call this *What is So, So What, What is Next?* To be able to live within each moment of time is where joy and empowerment is found. Be like a child who makes every moment count, fully engaged in the moment. It is the very reason why as you get older you perceive time to be slipping away more quickly; whereas, when you were a child a day seemed so eventful and long, summers felt like summer not just a quick break, and your days were created one moment at a time. Do not wish a moment away! Or shall I say savor the moment!

Abundance or Lack

Abundance is synonymous with alignment of your pure potential. It is important that you understand the distinction between abundance and lack and how it relates to you; hence my continuation of the discussion. Abundance is possibility thinking, my life is good and my future will be good. Knowing you are unique and infinite in your power to consciously create and love. Re direct your energy and thoughts upon creating, dreaming and living fully. Scarcity or lack is necessity and logical thinking, taking in life only as *What is So* rather than *What Can Be*. Too busy worrying about the future to live now only to feel behind and stressed for what is to come. Scarce energy and thinking are focused on surviving, worrying, hoarding, constricting, small thinking, and comparison to others. Scarcity and lack trigger a competitive mindset, where there is only one winner, and if it happens to be someone else who wins this means less for you; you lose.

Consider the scenarios of someone you know who: met the man of her dreams, less good men for you; promoted or new career means fewer opportunities for you; another's financial abundance means less money for you. When someone creates success in their life and you wish them well perhaps the thought has entered your mind, I want them to do well but not at the expense of my welfare. Or a colleague gets a promotion, recognition and the spotlight and you think only one person can have all the success, as if she is breathing your air leaving you polluted, stale sips of air. Can you begin to imagine the internal chaos this can cause? Or perhaps someone who is put together and has a good quality of life reminds you of your potential and whether you are living at your full potential or not as you observe her; you can allow it to debilitate or inspire your potential within. A lack mindset is constantly monitoring, controlling being dependent upon everyone else in the world, city, company, family, to await the result of will she or will she not get my Good Life leaving me with less. Also known as survival scarcity mode, thinking so small that you are worrying and focused on the external world leaving no energy for who really matters, the abundant you.

To be inspired is to be "In Spirit" and "Breath" in the Latin root, the very thinking you need to be alive for your well being, how then can you be inspired if you have a constant thought that someone else may be taking the air you breath, your spirit? This thinking only leaves you with a fear of dying which is really a false fear. As if to think there is a finite supply of everything when in truth there is an infinite source of well being. A reminder to you that empowerment is a natural never ending resource. You have access to an infinite source of creation by conspiring with the Universe knowing thoughts become materialized into things, emotions and experiences. Thoughts are limitless; therefore, creation and supply are limitless, be intentional with your thoughts for abundance to show her pretty face in your life today which will attract more for you to tomorrow.

So you can see how a scarcity mentality debilitates and has you frozen in pain. A scarcity mentality requires a lot of energy similar to having an identity that is not aligned with the grandest vision of you. With an identity of one who lives by the mantra *Get to Good* scarcity or lack would never make up the qualities you long for in turn abundance and inspiration may be ones you would like to magnify. Patience Grasshopper . . . I will talk more on identity in the section called Good on You.

Lack mentality has you sizing up the situation, evaluating in your head and comparing self to all that is external. You are unique; you were not created as a clone for comparison but like a snowflake one of a kind, pure with purpose.

Abundance is a reflection of your highest self. Co-creation and collaboration are abundant, formless into form. It will be helpful to remember that competition is scarcity, not enough in the world, I better get mine while I can at any cost before it is too late. A competitor says there can only be one winner and so it has you looking over your back wondering if someone is gaining on you and if you might be the loser. A creator says if I can imagine it I can create it, there is infinite supply and my creation does not destroy another it complements and contributes. Being a creator activates effortless prosperity for you are spending your energy on believing in your dreams and acting upon them. Quiet confidence is another trait exemplifying abundance. ***Think talents best utilized.*** While there may be many logical reasons not to believe in your dreams there only needs to be one reason to believe; make this the place your mind calls home. The Universe will conspire with you according to your beliefs and purpose in life. Think big and you get to play big on the planet. Let your motto be ***co-create rather than compete.*** Being a competitor is exhausting, who is out to get you, who do you need to outwit to get what you want, who do you have to convince that you are the best or what do you have to protect are just a few examples of a competitor's mindset.

Oh I do like abundance and I highly recommend you re read the section on abundance for there is a lot of opportunity for you to shift your thinking for creating an abundant world. Allow me to remind you of all that you are for who you is worthy nothing more needs to happen for you to claim abundance. You have the power to shift your mindset. *Get to Good Lifestyle Conditioning: Practice emitting abundant thoughts throughout your day and watch what happens.*

Abundance has also been thought of in the same context as prosperity. Prosperity can reference an abundance of money, health, relationships or anything you long for and value. Money is energy! What is the energy of your bank account? Currency in the Latin root "To Flow." Is money flowing toward or away from you? Is wealth circulating in your life? One definition of a Blessing can also be considered good fortune. Are you open to receive and allow blessings in your life? Do you feel blessed or cursed, blessed or burdened?

If you come from a lack mindset then you can expect your bank account to reflect accordingly. I need money comes with the afterthought of the absence of money so can you imagine why the stress and absence continues? If you notice yourself saying any of the following phrases on a consistent basis or your standard reply is: It is too expensive, I am broke, I do not have enough money, I cannot afford it, I do not have enough time, time is passing too quickly, I wish, Yes it would be nice to have that life, the rich just keep getting richer, look at her so materialistic, I will have to pass, not this year, life is hard to name a few then you are demonstrating a lack mentality. Coming from lack is choosing to be powerless over your world. No matter your current situation every one of us, right now can afford a shift in mindset. **While your choices of action may be minimal your choice of thought is not.** Your higher self is unaffected by such small thinking. You were born with greatness and an eternal spirit; lack has nothing to do with who you are. You added lack all on your own and you have the power to subtract it forever.

Bills are real, paychecks are real but you do not have to get stuck in a reality of pain. Create a new reality for yourself one where you take stock of an honest assessment of what percentage of time and energy do you give to lack and the same for abundance? While it may be considered crazy and illogical to believe beyond what is so you will only get more of what is if you avoid looking at what you want. Abundance begins and ends with you.

Now remember you get whatever you focus upon whether you want it or not. Abundant or lack mentality has you view and experience the world from much different perspectives. Which one are you including in your thinking? How do I know if I am offering an abundant mindset? Do you feel good? If yes then you are being abundant if not *Get to Good*. Practice the mantra **Get to Good** and you will access abundance.

A snapshot featuring Abundant and Lack Mentality

Abundant	Lack
All that I Am	All that I Am Not
All that I want	All that I do not want
All that I desire	All that I do not desire
All that I have	All that I do not have
All that is good	All that is less than good
All that is right	All that is wrong
Congruent	Contradiction
Harmony	Discord
Possibility	Necessity
Aligned	Misaligned
Collaborative	Competitive
Co-Creation	Separate
Infinite	Finite
Magnetic Pull	Forced Push
Compelling Future	Repelling
Moving Toward Pleasure	Moving away from pain

Alignment

Alignment is where you get everything you want. ***The answers you are seeking come from alignment.**** Your VIP Pass to the good life as defined by you. Alignment is synonymous with *Get to Good*. For if you feel good then you are in alignment. This is why feeling good transcends logic and reality. If you will fine tune your feelings toward good then you will allow good in kind. Alignment is the relationship between you and you. In other words, it is the relation between you and your Higher Self, Divine, God, Spiritual Self, Inner Being, Soul or your name of preference. Where are you in relation to how your Higher Self sees you and how you see you?

One who is aligned is more powerful than one billion who are not! Alignment is abundant, for it only considers the all inclusive good. ***Nothing more needs to happen to be worthy**,* go ahead and claim it. ***You never need to justify your existence.**** Once you get just how powerful you truly are, *and you will,* alignment will be of greatest importance to you.

While alignment is the invisible part of you it is complemented by the visible creation of your world. Your internal world projects upon your external world. If you are projecting alignment than you can expect for your life to be a reflection according to abundance. If you are out of alignment then your external world will too be a match for misalignment, similar to the mainstream saying "out of line." It all begins with you! Your materialized world begins within you as alignment. To know that all creation or what is to come originates with alignment is not to be taken lightly. Desires realized or not all comes down to you being in alignment. Alignment is not action or work;

it is you in relation to you. Now you can exhale knowing that you do not have to work so hard rather give more attention to how you feel and what you think, this would be a paradigm shift in working smarter not harder. Alignment allows you to access your power to tap into your potential, align yourself with higher self, and conjure with the Universe for an abundant return. **You are the ultimate return on investment.**

Your world as a reflection of aligned or misaligned energy shows up in your relationships, health, finances, career, spirituality, contribution to the world and well being. Not choosing alignment would be like asking a fish not to swim, lips not to kiss, you not to become. It goes against your abundant nature of well being and becoming.

Are you in a state of alignment? Do you feel good? Remember it is a yes or no answer anything more is a sophisticated excuse. *Feeling good trumps sophisticated excuses every time, no matter what.*

If the answer is yes then get to know this place you call feeling good and expand upon it, self mastery of your feelings is a worthy cause. If the answer is no then ask another question: How can I feel good? What is good in my life? What or who do I love? Very soon if not already you will be in a place of alignment for allowing all that is good and from this position inspired ideas and experiences will continue to present themselves to you. Mastering your personal alignment simply because it feels so good is the insider secret to the good life. Alignment is an elevated state of consciousness with personal access to a natural state of euphoria, known as High Vibration. It is available to you right now.

Again *Get to Good* is synonymous with alignment. Here is what you need to know regarding *Get to Good* it comes without conditions, contingencies or rules for accessing good. It does not matter the path you choose to *Get to Good*, or how you *Get to Good* so long as you *Get to Good!* It goes without saying that it will be a way that serves you and others while you *Get to Good*, the call is that you allow for it in the moment anywhere anytime with anyone. With *Get to Good* Lifestyle Conditioning you will have infinite ways to call upon it at will. Right now your focus is to ask the questions and explore ways that serve you for feeling good now. Only you will know if you feel good, have fun with it, you cannot get it wrong and there is no better time than this moment to feel good. Everything you desire is waiting for you to be aligned so you can allow it into your experience. Oh! Co-Creation at its finest moment!

Alignment is all about you! You 1st and while some may consider this selfish, new territory, foreign or egocentric, actually it is quite the opposite. For you cannot give away that which you do not have, if you do not fill yourself up with good then you have nothing good to offer anyone else. Think in this order of priority albeit not always convenient it will always serve you and anyone who has the privilege to be in your presence: Woman, Wife, Mother or Man, Husband, Father; a Mother cannot give fully to her child if she is out of alignment, just like a Husband cannot be fully available to his wife if he is out of alignment. You cannot feel bad enough to help another, sick or poor enough to serve this world. Your purpose is to go forth as an aligned being creating, expanding and experiencing the abundance that is circulating in your life. By doing this you then grant others permission to do so in kind. You empower rather than enable simply by choosing the mantra *Get to Good* as a lifestyle.

Alignment is a combination of your thoughts and feelings called vibration. Feeling good allows for good thoughts. Thoughts become things. Another way to look at alignment is vibration. A Good Vibe is lingo that is spoken in the mainstream while vibration may have been reserved for non secular settings and your inner stream. Beyond semantics, they both reference the same thing, an emission of energy. Being we are more of vibrational beings rather than verbal beings, you want to be in tune with the vibration you are emitting. What signal are you sending out with your thoughts and feelings? Do you want the same to boomerang back into your life disguised in circumstance?

The circumstance of life can be all consuming and so we forget to look at the cause. Like the Law of Cause and Effect, your Vibration causes an effect (life circumstance; people, places, things, events, and experiences.) Many times it does not appear related you wake up feeling off, anything but good and allow it to perpetuate throughout the day and you wonder why you spill coffee on your shirt, the project is put on hold, the car refuses to start, you fight with your husband or you just feel plain exhausted. Go back to the cause of it all, you allowed low vibration to set the tone for your day and you gave that more of the attention than noticing you felt less than good and choosing to *Get to Good!*

No one said you needed to be perfect and flawless without ever having a bad feeling thought, what is being said is get conscious to your vibration and be willing to shift in the moment and *Get to Good*. Not perfectly simply potentially. Believe me I would have been voted off the island a long time ago if perfection was the standard. Of course this is not rocket science; however it is the key to everything, do not dismiss the simplicity of a *Get to Good* shift. A positive shift in this moment attracts the next moment. Allow alignment to be a reminder of what you do want and how you want to feel rather than the lack mentality of all that you do not want. You can shift your consequence of what is to come with a *Get to Good* Vibration now.

Decisions are reflections of our vibration. You take decisions based upon your level of thinking and feeling. If you are aligned then you offer inspired decisions and action; if not you may procrastinate, decide out of fear, or react negatively. *Who shows up in life is based upon your vibration.* Aligned decisions allow for bigger thinking beyond circumstance allowing creative collaboration and inspired action. So many of you are so busy doing that you lose sight of being. You think let me go do today, check off my list, get it done and then maybe if I have time I will look at who I am. At the end of the day we ask what did I do today rather than who was I today?

What if you took on the decision to *Align then Act*? Alignment is the a majority of the action, while not a true mathematical equation, what if you looked at Alignment being 90% of your *Doing* today and 10% is you living out the inspired action? Might make for a much better day, more fulfilling, something left over in you at the end of the day where you fall to be victorious rather than depleted. There is not enough action in the world to make up for you being out of alignment. You cannot do your way into alignment and the good life. You can however *Get to Good* and then move through your day with inspired action and effortless prosperity.

Mastering your vibration is where you want to concentrate for it is in haphazard vibrational offerings where you can get confused as to why life is less than you had planned. Getting to know you, when you feel good, what needs to happen in order to feel good, and ways for feeling good is key for allowing your potential to come out and play. Most of you may not know when you feel good or how to feel good but you are certainly clear about what upsets you and what you do not like or want. Shift your thinking toward attention that is worthy of you: Being aligned in this moment. Take the contrast of what you do not like and use it to fine tune more of what you do like, personal preferences, turn the frequency dial from static contrast into fine tuned desires.

A clue into haphazard vibrational offering looks like the one eyed meditation, where you think you are going to multi task your day and get the result you want. While multi tasking may be fine for small portions of your day, the majority of your day would never need to call upon multi tasking as a way of getting everything done when you choose alignment first. I know some of you are not going to like or agree with this; however, if you have ever thought is there all there is, is this my life, I wish I had more time, when will my dreams come to pass, why me? Well then it might be time to give more attention to Alignment than your "to do" list, you will be pleasantly surprised about who shows up to the day and what manifests. *Find significance in mastering your alignment not your actions.*

Your getting things done has nothing to do with action, it is your vibrational offering that is of utmost importance. You cannot overcompensate with enough action for being out of alignment. Even if it has proven results in the past, it is usually at the expense of self compromise. Your abundant life is an emotional journey not an action journey. Get in the habit of checking in with your vibration (thoughts and feelings) first and often then move with inspired action. Alignment is tapping into the invisible that if you are willing can work in concert with you for creating the day you love rather than waiting for one day. Alignment for the pure sake of alignment is the order of the day. Desires manifested come from alignment. My intent is to bring you inspiration and great comfort in knowing that you can shift your vibration at any time and that the majority of action today takes place within you as alignment. Knowing you are powerful and complete is comforting. *I Am Worthy and All is Well.* Get to know this natural place, allow it to be your sacred space for living as the person you were intended to be and embrace the call to be more. We are Human Beings not human doings. What will you conjure up for your day by choosing alignment first and foremost? Who will allow into your sphere of influence? Who will you become at the end of today? *Anticipate something great is about to happen.*

Vibrational Match

You are saying it but are you feeling it? Saying one thing and thinking and feeling another is incongruent with being a match to your desires. While emotions do not create, they are your signal, announcement, whisper for letting you know in what direction you are moving, good or not so good, abundance or scarcity. You say you want money, love and joy but are you feeling it, what is the unsaid vibration you are offering? When you think of money what comes up for you stress or anticipation? If you are in question or spinning it then peak into your bank account for it will reflect which feeling you have been giving more attention to because abundance is an emotional journey. The same is true for any of your desires, you want them but how do you feel about your wanting them?

Contrast of what you do not want provides you with an opportunity to fine tune your desires and become a match. When you think of what you want in life and even for your day today allow the emphasis to be upon what would I need to think and feel in order to be a vibrational match for my desire? For my belief to be in synch with my desires, for it to compel rather than repel, permit rather than postpone, is it a match? If a belief or mantra is a conditioned thought then what thought would be congruent with your desire? You may want something but if your belief is a contradiction then you will keep it outside your experience. You cannot offer a vibrational contradiction and expect the Universe to play in harmony with you; they do not match up, which one of these things is not like the other? What I want and what I believe are to be in harmony not discord. Again no amount of action will make up for a contradictory belief. On the other note, a congruent belief will be enough to allow inspired living as an attractive force for your desire. I call this effortless prosperity or accelerated abundance. It is available to you right now with a shift toward *Get to Good* vibration.

What is the unspoken vibration you are emitting? Notice if the unspoken vibration is congruent with the spoken word. The unsaid is more important than the said remember integrity being what I want is how I feel. It would be better to feel it than say a word.

If when your desire shows up and you say, "What took you so long, I thought you would never come?" Your Desire will say, "I know that is what took me so long." Mindful of the all inclusive Universe, abundant in nature, only saying YES to you and your desires. The Universe does not discriminate in your favor or against you. She does not say "Oh she has been through so much in her life already let us give her a break, or she really is a good person or he has been wild let us have him repent a little longer for his past mistakes. The contradiction is omitted in the Universe when you say I do NOT want . . . . the only thing that is received is I do want. This is why it is important that you give attention to that which you DO WANT rather than all that you Do Not Want. The Universe is responding to your vibration (thoughts and feelings.) Only you say No to self not the Universe, she is on your side, your raving fan, if you will allow it by taking the time to line up your energy with your desires and live from alignment. Are you holding your hand up in a stop position or waving desires on in with your vibration? Alignment transcends logic and time; think of it as accelerated abundance.

It is all relative, the relation between you and your desires or stated another way your desires and your beliefs. You have to be willing to be honest with your current belief system. Consider this, you can look at a person's life on the outside and notice the correlation between their external world and internal world. Look at the results of your life today, your body, bank account, relationships, and career and with precision know if you have been emitting good feeling thoughts or not. It is not a trick, nor is their room for error in the formula of think and feel good allow good; think and feel less than good and allow less than good. Again the question posed to you is: What have you been thinking? How have you been feeling? Does it serve you? **The Universe is the original matchmaker.**

Get to Good Lifestyle Snapshot

Wellness

Let us look at your health and body, if you feel good with your health and body then continue to give it the priceless attention it deserves. If you eat a dessert, enjoy it; allow your body to assimilate it based upon your feeling good while eating it rather than the nutritional content. Does this mean eat only desserts or desserts everyday, only you can decide, but what happens to those who are aligned and feeling good about their body, is they tend to take decisions that honor their body rather than self sabotage. Consider this, you would be better off eating a cupcake and savoring it than eating a salad and complaining. I know the green light I just gave everyone to go out for cupcakes tonight, remember alignment first then act on cupcake or empowering alternative.

Your body is a visible representation of your collective thoughts. When you are ill or tired, your body is signaling to you that you are out of alignment. For some of you, it only needs to be the beginning of a scratchy throat and you realize balance is needed while others of you will let it get to a diagnosis before you will wake up to the message your body is sending you and even then some get so caught up in the label of the diagnosis that you become the illness rather than the aligned person. Well being is the nature of your body, ease and vitality; dis ease is your body indicating misalignment. Alignment allows for Mind Body and Spirit to be in synch with who you are and the choices you make to honor your body. The best kept anti aging secret is well being for your body responds favorably. For when you feel good you look good. Here is a vibrational belief that would serve you well: *My Body is A Temple!* Imagine the way you would feel and the nutrition and exercise choices you would give yourself thinking from this elevated mindset?

Relationships

We are all interconnected and play an important role for defining who we are and what we want. The relationship between You and Your Higher Self is most important. When you bring an aligned you to the conversation with others you contribute a priceless gift. What would your relationships (professional, personal and intimate) say about who you have chosen to be lately? What you have been contemplating about who is in your life? Harmony or discord inside a relationship can be traced back to you and your vibration (thoughts and feelings.) Compliment or complaint, fulfilled or drained, connection or competition? Who is circulating in your life? Who do you continue to invite into your private life? I always attract the guy who is non committal, passive aggressive or immature. Well then, *It Is So.* She thinks it, feels it and believes it then he must show up into her life. Some of you will overcompensate with action to make him or her want to love you out of the need to please and make the love last. While the intent may be good, you end up *doing love* rather than *being love* with the contingency upon more action required to keep the love coming and going for approval. If you did not make another your reason for being out of alignment you would be liberated to be you. *Personal Alignment is . . . Happily Ever After!*

Perhaps a better way to look at an intimate relationship is: Who do I want in my life, what do I want in a relationship and how can I be a vibrational match to him or her? Think of a relationship match as a complement to accenting the greatness in yourself and another. If you find yourself thinking I wish he or she loved and respected me more, then it is your role to become a match to love and respect not wait until the evidence of him or her loving you shows up. A Mentor of mine says it profoundly "participate in your own rescue." Inside a relationship with discord there is a tendency to blame the other person for the majority of the wrongdoing. And while this may feel like you are off the hook, the truth is it only puts you in a holding pattern outside of alignment far from your potential individually and collectively inside the relationship. When you truly get that the other person is off the hook of your happiness you are free to be without judgment, withholds or resentment. This applies to all relationships whether it is your spouse, partner, boss, co worker, business partner, employee, driver on the highway, sales associate, person sitting next to you on the airplane, or barista brewing your latte. You are not here to control another nor do you want to be controlled. Your power comes into play with your response to another, it is a choice to show up powerfully or powerless.

I have been with my husband for almost half my life so I can certainly speak to the magical and unbecoming moments. For fulfilling relationships implement *Get to Good lifestyle conditioning:*

1. Become a match to your desired relationship
2. Amplify 1-2 qualities you admire in the other person
3. Do not let another be your reason for not being aligned. Be aligned no matter what.

Finances

What does your financial portfolio say about you and your thoughts? Do you speak of the lack of money, cannot afford mindset, and debt that you may have accrued? Money is Energy! Are you compelling or repelling; what is your Financial Vibration? Prosperity is an emotional journey. While most of have been taught that wealth is attributed to hard work, luck or class, abundance responds to your consistent thoughts and feelings you have about money. The same energy required to create $100 is equal to the same energy required to create $1 Million; it is all a matter of your belief and intention. So have you made money friend or foe, extended a deliberate invitation or retract every time a bill or expense shows up? No matter the reason you may have kept finances at bay whether brought up to think money is bad, you have to work hard, not for everyone, never had it so never will; you can shift the flow of money into your life with *Get to Good*.

You may be saying you want more money but how do you feel when you say it? Contradictory vibrations will never match your desire for money. A talking head does not make for a desire realized, better to feel it than say a word. Again abundance is the order of the Universe; you either believe you too are included in the line up or you take yourself out of the equation by not allowing yourself to feel good when it comes to money. What if you gave bills a new meaning from pain or lack to choice and commitment? For instance, when you pay your auto loan rather than thinking of it as a negative remember most of you chose your car because you liked it or thought it was a fit for you, why feel bad about making good on your realization? Seems like a contradiction that will only perpetuate more contradictory circumstances in your life unless you shift your thinking and perceptions. While smart to reduce expenses it is wiser to give the majority of your attention toward expansion. Perhaps for some of you feeling good about money at the time is a stretch and inauthentic then *Get to Good* about anything or anyone in your life unrelated to money. Take your attention off money and place it upon that which does allow for good. You would be better served with your financial status in your singing out loud than in your crunching numbers one more time. Put the calculator down please.

Get to Good Lifestyle Conditioning:

1. Practice the feeling of abundance throughout the day
2. Notice and say *thank you* or *of course* to the evidence of abundance in your day
3. Enjoy joyfully giving intangibly and tangibly

Career as Calling

What do you want to be when you grow up? Having purposeful thoughts allows for A Calling rather than a job or career whether you are still in school or in the workforce. Do your beliefs support you in discovering, learning and attracting an aligned career? For some of you Motherhood is your full time calling, make no apology for this higher calling you have chosen, your contribution to this world is not taken lightly and I applaud you. For others the complaint of your current career overshadows your thoughts for the ideal career. If you were to reinvent your career, what would you do and what would you need to think and feel about it to create a calling? No need to exit your current position until you line up with what you want; otherwise, you will create the same scenario simply under a new position. Remember your boss, co workers and school are off the hook of your success. Have you subscribed to the norm of I hate Mondays and TGIF, how much life are you missing by thinking this way? How can you live a day well lived today, what would you need to think and expect? Today no matter the day of the week is full of abundance and possibility, will you show up powerfully and aligned or wish it away?

Turn your career into your calling and you never have to work another day again. Do what you love and love what you do. Turn your passion into your career and you will attract prosperity, joy and purpose. Successful enterprise today calls upon abundant mentality for collaboration and creation. A visionary focuses beyond what is and gives attention upon what is beyond. You can find bigger meaning in any line of work, in your current position, or perhaps it is time to live into a new career. If it is just a means to an end then it is not your calling and you have access to living your calling. Creating a life purpose grander than you allows the passion to pull you into a bigger role. *Think inspiration rather than obligation.* When the intent of your calling is "To Serve" then you know you are in alignment with the grandest vision of you.

Well Being

All is Well is another mantra worth considering. I often refer to the saying "Patience Grasshopper." It is a place of peace, quiet confidence and clarity. What would the conversation in your head say about the level of well being you allow in your private thoughts? This is the most important dialogue you will have all day, is it inspiring, empowering, uplifting and encouraging? Remember I get whatever I think about whether I want it or not; What do I want? Who do I want to be? How do I want to feel?

My sisters and I have an inside joke which I suppose you are now part of the inner circle if you like, anytime we are not allowing well being and giving more attention to stress our eyes begin to twitch. We call any stressful scenario an "eye twitcher" so if you see me and I am incessantly winking at you it may be your time to come up and remind me to breathe. I now know that if my eye begins to twitch it is my signal that I am offering a vibration that is out of alignment with who I am and it is my time to *Get to Good*. I told you my halo slipped daily. So I simply adjust it rather than think "just my luck" and complain that I must have been given a defective halo. Otherwise it is a misuse of personal power. Your body is so wise, it signals to you the thoughts you have been thinking, do not take the signals lightly rather use them as a gauge for alignment.

Well being is absent drama, chaos or resistance and this may be new to a few of you. Some of you have become so comfortable with a dramatic life that you think it is protocol for the day. Leave drama for Hollywood, allow yourself a stage of well being to experience places both emotionally and physically from an elevated position. Well being will flow over into all areas of your life from your health, finances, relationships, calling and your world. One affects the other; allow it to serve you and others. Breath is one of the quickest ways to access well being, deep abdominal breathing, take three and notice the immediate shift in your vibration. **News Flash:** everywhere you go there you are, with whomever you are with and whatever you are experiencing; why not breathe in well being? Well being is a state of mind not a destination. How wonderful to know that the person you are going to be spending the day with will be in a state of well being, that you are privileged to spend the day with you, A VIP. **Be Well.**

Parenting

The greatest gift you can offer a child is one of alignment, first yours then creating a sacred space for child to get to know her personal alignment. Children are the closest to God, they are jumping off a much higher stage than the generation before; for example they are skilled on technology without the need for direction and we are shocked and still trying to figure it out ourselves, my advise: simply ask a child for help. If trusted with personal accord children would continue to live in alignment joyfully learning with wonderment. As parents and adults, we tend to interfere, think we have all the answers and impose our beliefs upon children. Please do not confuse this with an expectation for respect and honor from your child as Mother and Father, you being aligned will only be a match for honor and received in kind.

Perhaps it is a paradigm shift with the parent being in awe of the child, creating a sacred space for the child to express freely who she is and what she prefers. Get curious, ask questions, telling is not compelling; create a space for empowerment for your child to step into willingly and joyfully. While I am over the moon about all that my Princess is I give more attention to how she thinks and feels about herself and her world, this is creating a sacred space for accessing personal alignment beyond her years at home. As a Mother that feels good serving her of the highest good. I know I am blessed having one of the greatest Mothers in the world, my Mom always communicates from a space of believing in all that I am. I let her know just how much her love means to me and how appreciative I am for her and my sisters who are my confidants and raving fans. Who in your family can you share your appreciation, family being defined by you?

My daughters' favorite phrases are *Easy or Oh Great I Love That*; we have linked that way of being to alignment. Along with using her name synonymous with personal alignment, I notice her feeling good and reference her name for instant recall and expectation; "I see you are showing up as (child's name) does that feel good? That is personal alignment, you are so powerful." And yes speak powerfully to your children, they are better equipped to absorb big words and ideas than anyone else you will be spending time with today, be impressed by their brilliance and example of possibility calling you to be more in kind. Over the past year, my daughter has been intent on writing Dear Santa letters requesting A Real Magic Wand. I have let her know the power of her mind being her magic wand but she wants nothing to do with that conversation. Mommy, not the mind again. Ok I say, "God has placed a real magic wand in your heart." She looks at me without skipping a beat and declares "Well, I wish he would have placed it in my hands." Oh My Stars! This is the same Princess who calls me to be more while becoming an Author at age 4 on her own accord before her Mommy. A tall order in my world please send me Good Vibes.

Think co creation as Parent and Child. How do you see your child, capable or dependent? What message are you sending out to your child on a daily basis? As a parent are you saying without words: I believe in you and your potential or something less? It is not too late; you can begin today speaking from your potential to hers.

No matter the age you are a child of God and have an inner child who longs to come out and play. Many of you have chosen not to allow yourself to play for you are consumed with telling the story of your rotten childhood, please tell me what is the statute of limitations for blaming your parents for your adult life?

Parenthood is a privilege, a tall order, where alignment is mirrored and magnified; it shows up in magical moments observing and being with your child or unbecoming moments such as tantrums in the middle of the shopping mall to teenagers acting out to seek attention. As I reread these words, they are quite telling with my experience as a Mother this morning and such a good reminder for me. As the Author I promise I am commanding of myself that which I am sharing with you. Children are seeking approval from their parents, if you will turn the thinking upon their own personal approval and compassion for others there will be fewer tendencies for insecurity and disempowerment allowing more personal power for your child. Begin to associate parenting to alignment and you will be amazed of the positive influence you have upon your child. As a parent, you can set the tone for alignment for your child and household, your child will model your favorable or questionable behavior for you are the Hero and Goddess in her eyes. Sharing love, wisdom and guidance from an aligned space is the parent handbook. What is the greatest gift you could ever give your child? Beyond material possessions and life experiences it is the gift of her knowing and allowing personal alignment, the consistent message being *you are loved and worthy.*

Imagine the world being a better place having your aligned child come out and play? Priceless! A heartfelt Thank you!

Global Beliefs

Consider widely used phrases that while acceptable among society are in vibrational discord with desire: Par for the course, what else could go wrong, this always happens to me, what could be next, welcome to my world, see what I have to deal with on a daily basis, what now, or I knew this would happen. Or take into consideration global metaphors like: When it rains it pours, waiting for the other shoe to drop, the story of my life, or one bad apple spoils the bunch. Truly nothing acceptable about these vibrations, all are declaring lack mentality having nothing to do with who you are and what you want. Why be right about all that is wrong? Here is the enlightening message of those phrases, they work, your thought truly is your invitation, you are calling into your experience that which you contemplate. Perhaps it is time to give more of your concentration to elevated thoughts for allowing them to work in concert with your desires.

Here are some elevated metaphors or vibrational beliefs that you may want to consider *"I feel like a million bucks, The world is my playground, and Everything I touch turns to gold."* We are either more committed to our stance or committed to live by the mantra *Get to Good!* One proposes more of the same while the other prospers beyond what is.

Here is where conspiring with The Universal Laws and Faith play a vital role in your life, when you feel aligned as a vibrational match *before* your desire manifests. Where you do not need to see it to believe it, you need to think it and feel it and then you will see it. Do I feel good? Yes, then I will bring about my desires, stay here and enjoy simply feeling good. Here is my promise, if you remain intent upon *Get to Good* the desire will be realized. Be good to yourself, honest with your vibration and willing to get out of your own way, get off it and *Get to Good!*

Alignment for the sake of alignment is the breath of life. You are unattached and unaffected by anything outside of you all the while creating your desires from a state of pure joy, ease and fun. Why do you think you chose to come here, for pain or pleasure? No one would sign up for a lifetime of pain, let your thoughts be worthy of you. Permission granted.

On Purpose

Begin to dream bigger for the Universe will meet you in direct proportion to your desires. Why not call yourself to be more? You are going to be thinking anyway; may as well think big? What percentage of my day is devoted to my desires? Amplify this percentage and allow it to grow exponentially in your life. Notice when you are off and without criticism or upset simply *Get to Good!* For you to notice how you feel is the power place, then you have conscious choice in the matter, for you to think I cannot do this, it is too hard, I messed up again, I am not sure of this lends itself to less than good. Do not spend time here, celebrate you noticed and shift to good in the moment. In the near future as you implement *Get to Good Lifestyle Conditioning* you can expect your lag time between not so good and good to shorten simply with a breath and a mantra.

What will you Desire? If you were to reinvent, rediscover or fine tune your world, what would you desire? What beliefs, conditioned thoughts, would you want to have supporting you on your journey?

Most people will allow themselves to dream only to a certain point. The stopping point is when a person gets to the "How" will I make my dreams come true. Thinking on a liner scale, point A to point B, has you thinking logically and action oriented whereas thinking on an exponential scale has you transcend logic and move toward your dreams with inspired action on purpose. When you feel like you have to figure out the details of how, who, what, where and when first then you minimize the desire and amplify the details (and this never feels good hence leaving you out of alignment.) The How can be very limiting and all limitations are self imposed. When you know the WHY or the purpose the how will follow with ease and joy. As you Dream, follow this sequential order for manifesting your desires: WHO, WHAT, WHY, and ELEVATED HOW. The Who is YOU, aligned abundant all that I am, the What is What do I want, clarity on desires, the Why is the purpose behind the what and the Elevated How is the inspired action complementing the abundant emotional journey. Not only will you be inspired to realize your dreams you will enjoy the path along the way which will be important for being a vibrational match to your dreams. I call this an adrenaline rush, not knowing how it will all unfold but knowing I will be there and it will be better than expected.

Get to Good Lifestyle Conditioning:

Who am I?
What do I want?
Why do I want it?
What inspired action can I take?

You have innate potential, when you feel pain it is your potential aching to come out and play. If you have been postponing your potential then the Universe or life has ways of stretching you to call yourself to be more that may be uncomfortable and inconvenient. It is those moments where you know better whether in your career, relationships, health or money and you push through it anyway and try and make it happen. It is where circumstance shows up as a reminder that you are to be aligned and the only thing worthy of your attention is a shift toward *Get to Good.* Many of you have remained status quo or over stayed your welcome in different areas of your life and a call to be more is the only solution. Perhaps use one of my personal mantras **Leave the party when you are having fun.** (leave postponement and allow potential) It does not have to get to this point, if you will only recognize that alignment is priority and living a life according to your alignment is the original purpose of life. Decisions, behavior and action all flow from your relativity of alignment. What decision will you take today that is a reflection of your potential? Dream big for a compelling future that keeps you up late and wakes you up early for living a day well lived.

The pain you feel is your purpose aching to break free so you can be fully alive. For those of you waiting until all is perfect in your world before you bring purpose to your life know you are only delaying passion. It is the minutia that has you preoccupied so passion and purpose take a back seat, giving more emphasis on not now . . . once I have more money saved . . . as soon as the children are grown . . . as soon as my business is in order . . . and time has a funny way of continuing on while we do this thing called life.

Just get me to the weekend so I can relax, wishing away life only to escape. What if you loved your life that you did not want to escape? You anticipated today with an expectation that something good was going to happen knowing tomorrow will get here on its own time. To be able to say My Life is Good! I Love My Life! What will it take for you to believe it and say it with conviction? Then claim it, what could you possibly be waiting for, more mediocrity, average routine living, playing big only compared to others? Consider this an intimate invitation to live by purpose, permission granted. Remember you are the creator of your experience, you have all the power to make your life the way you want it, so the question then is what do you want? Give attention only to that which you want, schedule your day accordingly where your lifestyle is a reflection of the abundant you and be the person you have always wanted to be today. No one else can do it for you, they can only reflect back to you the beliefs you have about yourself. You hold the key to unlock the good life.

When you were younger and dreamed of your life, is this the life you envisioned for yourself? What is different, better or worse? What did you believe in your younger years to know your dreams were possible for your life? What would you need to believe today to ignite your dreams for a life of passion and purpose again? Allow this to be a reminder of who you were intended to be. In order to dream, you must be willing to let go of the current circumstance of your life of what is so and think beyond. A compelling future brings purpose for today. To dream you must think bigger than the current inventory of your life. If you only take stock of *what is* you only create more of the same. Your current state of affairs does not have to be your consistent reality. *What is real? The place that holds your attention.* Transcend logic with thinking above and beyond current circumstance with creative thought. Telling it like *it is* only promotes more of *what is*.

Play the "Let's Pretend Game." If I had my life to live anyway my heart desired what would I do, what would it look like, what would the purpose of my life be? If you were able to travel into the future on a time machine and sneak a peak into you living your dreams what and who would you see? How would it make you feel knowing you have all this and more to look forward to for the life you created today? What words of wisdom and beliefs would your future self share with you? What if nothing changed today and you took a ride into the future, would you like who and what you see, would you look forward to the future created by you? You are a powerful person who has been given freedom to choose and create a life worthy of you. Take that same time machine and travel in the past to meet with that younger you, the one who had all the dreams and believed they were possible, what words of encouragement would the younger self say to you, what would be whispered in your ear so you would believe in your purpose forever unshakeable no matter the circumstances of events. What thoughts would your younger self believe? Reflect upon this and use it to be powerful beyond measure no matter your circumstance whether: same old same old, a diagnosis from your doctor, a business deal gone bad, single and searching, an unfulfilling marriage, married by paper alone, children who have taken the wrong path, overwhelming debt, life is good or I have a dream for the scenario may change but you do not have to compromise.

Thought leaders are visionaries; think embody and envision. Clarity comes from living a life of purpose. When you are clear you do not spend time dwelling upon all that is not good in your life or mediocre; you direct your energy toward your passion and purpose in life. Look for evidence of this in your day and you will find it. *Get to Good Lifestyle Conditioning: Visualize and Imagine more throughout your week.*

Permission granted to become a match to your desires. Permission granted declares I am worthy of my desires. Today I strolled Worth Avenue in Palm Beach or as I like to call it Worthy Avenue one of my favorite spots in the world because I use it as a *Get to Good* Lifestyle Conditioning for fine tuning my alignment. What is one of your favorite spots in the world? Mine all have to do with my best showing up or alignment not necessarily a destination but a mindset. I encourage you to get to know what feels good to you, become acquainted with the abundance that is yours, giving attention only to that which is worthy of you. *Get to Good lifestyle conditioning: End every thought with an elevated thought upon your desires.*

GOOD ON YOU

Identity is one of the strongest forces in human psyche. You will do more to remain consistent with the identity you hold for yourself. Two of the most powerful words in any language translate to **I AM**. When you say *I Am* your way of being is congruent with the identity you hold for yourself. Who you declare yourself to be will show up consistently in your life, beliefs, vibration, actions, decisions and manifestations. If asked the question: Who are you? How would you respond? Many might say your name then move on to your roles both personally and professionally. Hello my name is _____, I am a wife, mother, husband, business owner, entrepreneur, professional, or homemaker however you answered is true for you. Or you may include an emotion: I am stressed, busy, carefree, excited, curious, waiting, hopeful or anxious.

Identities can either call upon your potential or problems; they can be outdated, disempowering labels, or simply out of alignment with who you really are today. Or an identity can call you to be more: I am abundant, aligned, empowered, Goddess or Hero. Be mindful of the identity you hold for yourself and allow it to serve you in creating the life you desire. As your life evolves it is important to be mindful of identity so not to wake up one day and feel a loss of identity. A reinvention and reminder of identity is always a good idea in any phase of life.

Most claim identities, which fall under one or all of the following: one dimensional, standard, circumstantial, mediocre, out dated, or negative. *It is not what you are called but what you answer to that matters most.* If you do not decide upon your identity the external world will do it for you. Others may look upon you in a way that upholds you to a powerful identity while still others may look upon you that holds you to a lower standard. Whether your parents, spouse, boss, boyfriend, or acquaintance thinks one way of you need not be the standard for your thinking. Giving your power away to others for deciding who you are to be and your fate for decisions made from a disempowering identity is setting you up for failure. While it is rewarding to be favorably looked upon it can also be defeating when others look poorly upon you; in either case none are the powers of be, you are the only one who can access your greatness. If you believe in what others are saying about you and quiet your own internal voice then you allow them to shape and mold you either positively or negatively. If you turn the volume up on your own vibration then you are the one to consciously choose your identity leading to The Good Life declared by you. One who clams an empowering identity lives by the mantra *Get to Good.*

You know people who have chosen not to live into an empowering identity at times in their lives, perhaps you know this person intimately. Labels that have been given to those people who have a loss of identity resemble: poser, people pleaser, fake, phony, liar, big talker, lost, depressed, flakey, insecure, arrogant, martyr, victim and egocentric to name a few. Harsh labels yet true feelings for many who have encountered such people. So why would you avoid the truth of who you are and tolerate a less than way of being? Perhaps it is the fear of finding out who you really are and in the discovery of self what if you become a disappointment, then what? An illusion that you are unworthy of being thought of as brilliant for who you are, on your own without the accolades, material things, shallow words or empty promises. So you avoid unveiling the truth of your greatness for superficial cover up in the meantime. Posturing with others to meet a need of feeling significant, liked, and valued. All the while living from a false sense of security similar to the Emperor having no clothes. Longing for acceptance and approval by others never mind yourself, wanting to please others even at the risk of self compromise, hoping to fit in, hoping not to be found out, not sure of who you are, thinking it is the only way, not privy to listening to your highest self you push onward hoping to hold out a bit longer. Worried about what others think and say about you, likened perhaps to some of your childhood days on the playground circulating in your life again for the grown up you today. *When you attempt to be something to everyone you end up being nothing to anyone.*

This way of being is so exhausting, it is similar to telling a lie and this time the lie is being told by you to you over and over again. Humor me for a moment and pretend you have told a lie once in your life, how many more lies did it take to keep the original lie alive? More lies are needed to fuel the original lie and it does not stop there for it becomes perpetual and can lead to a way of being and acting. When we lie about who we are, we have to maintain that lie with so many false perceptions while denying the very greatness of our being. And at the end of the day, chances are you did not fulfill your promise, you were out of integrity, depleted, exhausted and stressed and thought of as either insecure or egocentric. Is this worth it? Was this your intention when you began to tell the lie of who you believe yourself to be and how you portray that to the world? It became skewed along the way for you chose to go to fear, pride or ego rather than love, honor and quiet confidence. Why make it so difficult on yourself and deny yourself the truth of you living as you? It is called The Naked Truth . . . if you eliminate all the fear who would you be left with right now? You and your higher self aka Alignment . . . would that be O.K.?

It has been said that who you are is the person who shows up when know one is looking. My husband said to me in the beginning of our relationship, *Jacqueline you will be rewarded in public that which you practice in private*. Mind you this is the same wise man who in my unbecoming moments has said *he now knows what the devil looks like.* It is good to be called to be more, certainly not always convenient but worthy. So if no one was looking would you behave that way, speak those words, think those thoughts or is it all for show? Remember the label Show Off; it was never associated with a good thing. Can you begin to see the viscous cycle occurring in your life if you go external first then bargaining with your internal? As if to negotiate with integrity to bend the rules a little bit just this time. And for what? Loss of self? Not you, no thank you!

You are more than your circumstance. Some say that our experiences define us while others believe who we are being in the experience defines our true character. Like the law of cause and effect, the superficial artificial you is present when you live at the effect, the authentic genuine you is eternal and present when you live from the cause. Declaring who we are is the defining moment in life. Declaration is to decide in advance. To decide who you will be in advance rather than wait for the world to tell you who you ought to be or how they interpret you to be. Integrity brings about dignity. *I Am* comes from within anything else is self compromise. Nothing needs to happen for you to declare **I AM** it is available to you right now no matter your life circumstance. When I appeared on a TV Show for Animal Planet I believe the original intent behind casting was the dichotomy of a petite metropolitan southern girl turned catfish cowgirl. Instead, I simply chose to bring Jacqueline to the filming which made for a much more fulfilling experience for crew, viewers and me. *You and the good life are not mutually exclusive.*

In this world of peace and chaos does anybody know where I can find myself? Here is where I know it cannot be found . . . self cannot be found in the next car you buy, next career move, negotiated big deal, special someone, spouse or children, it cannot be found in a dream home, bank account, holiday, chiseled abdominals or pint of gelato. Believe me I have embarked on many personal external expeditions and came up with empty treasure every time. Self is not something to be found outside of you it can only be found within you. As if by filling up with external stimuli you will find yourself or never have to come face to face with your true self. As a society we seem to be looking in unsuccessful places for finding self, yet place it in our hearts and we will never believe it.

Acquaint yourself with the best of you, aligned with *Get to Good* moments, and let this be a familiar place for your mind to rest upon rather than all that you are not. So many of you are looking outside of self for validation and you wonder why self esteem issues are prevalent in our society. It is no coincidence that the characteristic self esteem has the word self in it, it only has to do with self not someone else. Confidence and worthiness follow the same guidelines; you were born worthy you only discount it when you forget this truth. Forgetting who you are and losing yourself is a resignation to the greatness within you, remembering is honor. Consider this your gentle reminder.

Most people ask what did I do today? *Why not ask who was I today?* A paradigm shift for your day: Daily To Do List: #1 ALIGNMENT. *Get to Good Lifestyle Conditioning Question: When you put your head on the pillow tonight you can ask not just what did I do today but who was I today?*

BE while you DO allows you to access your highest self anywhere anytime. Making it happen at the expense of self is not making it happen, it is faking it. Remember this only leads to perpetual pain and frustration in your life.

Your need to remain consistent with the identity you hold for yourself is all pervasive. Your identity is reflective in your life in terms of how you think, act, decide, respond, set standards, believe, allow, and expect inside relationships, spirituality, health, career, family, finances, contribution and emotional well being. Who you say you are has a direct effect on both your internal and external world. So you can appreciate the importance your identity has on your life. Consider this the identity you hold for yourself determines your destiny. It is everything and it is you. You must begin with you first if you are going to create and live the life you have always dreamed. An aligned identity is an invitation to prosperity, love, abundance, and pure potential and infinite possibilities.

The identity you hold for yourself manifests in your daily life. Reflect upon the following questions and allow them to resonate for you: Does your current identity serve you? Does it bring out the best in you? Does it bring you closer to your dreams? Does it allow for you to be the one inspired to act upon your dreams? If your identity were to be a color then your world would be colored accordingly like the saying *paint the town red.* Your identity is an extension and reflection in your lifestyle. Is your identity based upon someone else's ideals or criticisms? Is your identity outdated? Are you still holding on to an identity from your school days, previous relationship, or prior career? Is your identity average, the norm or mediocre? There is a grander vision of you that is not limited by your past experiences or future worries, let go to make room for you uncompromised, you inspired. Perhaps now is a good time to recreate your identity. No matter your age or life experience, you are always seeking growth, so reinventing yourself rather than staying stale and stagnate is an opportunity worth claiming. *Get to Good* Identity Conditioning can be found in the section Ah The Good Life. Recreating your identity is an exciting time for it allows you to elevate your thinking and way of being. This may be that time for you.

My invitation to you is to call upon an empowering all pervasive identity capturing the essence of your spirit and a call to be more. Can you imagine what your life will be like if it is reflecting the grandest vision of you, living from alignment, absent of self compromise and the presence of dreams realized?

An aligned identity is quiet confidence, it is when you walk into a room and others think "I want that for me." No words are needed to exude God's gifts in you when you live from alignment within your identity. Whereas lack of self confidence or insecurity can show up as withdrawn, putting a wall up, disconnect, caddy or ego driven, the remedy is to align and

Get to Good. It is important to consciously choose your identity otherwise the external environment (people and circumstances) will influence who you are in every moment. This causes chaos and internal turmoil, like a leaf allowing the wind to blow it and fall where it may. Self-compromise is the loss of self, it is similar to saying I am person X when really you are person Z. Keep in mind the external world is everything and everyone outside of you, in the modern age our brains are receiving millions of bytes per second from external stimuli, all the more reason to declare an empowering identity in advance. Allowing the external world to influence you will only bring about disconnect on what is truth and what is an illusion.

Decisions you make all come from the identity you hold for yourself. Decisions determine your destiny, big and small. If life is made up of decisions and you are the decision maker, what is the quality of your decisions? How are your decisions shaping your life today? Take a picture of your life right now in all areas of your life, your emotional well being, spirituality, body and health, career, finances, relationships, and charitable efforts; do the current state of affairs reflect the grandest vision of you? If yes, congratulations on living from your truth, cheers to your evolvement. If the answer is no, understand that knowing allows you to do something about it now. You can begin to focus on what you would prefer when you take a snapshot of your life decisions and who must you be to create a life accordingly. Once you get clear on your identity all decisions will flow from this centered higher place, your higher self in action.

An empowering identity allows for decisions to come from your internal world then projected unto your external world. You can access effortless prosperity from this level of decision making. For when you know who you are life's decisions become clear and effortless. The lag time between a thought and a realized manifestation of that thought is shortened when you act from a higher place of being. Here is a clean example for you: I am a vegetarian, being this is one element of my identity not my all pervasive identity, making decisions as to what I eat come easily, anything with a face is never an option, doubt or bone of contention. The food I eat no matter at home, a restaurant, party or traveling are never compromised for I choose to be a vegetarian; therefore, I only eat foods which align with me being a vegetarian. Now if I said it would be nice to be a vegetarian, I would like to, I really should, I will look into it, I want to be a part of the trend then when it came time to decide what I will eat at a steak house, on the go lifestyle, or cocktail party I may be influenced by my external world to eat meat and then put off my being something I would like to be one more day or one more meal. Hereto the food choices would reflect the identity of not being a vegetarian yet causing me pain and disconnect for it is an identity taken on by default and lack of internal strength. In the first scenario one creates her world, in the second scenario one allows the world to create her; one is powerful with the other leaving one powerless. The truth is you are the creator of your experience and your identity, once you will realize this for yourself decisions will be clear and life reflects back to you your potential.

Who you declare yourself to be is not contingent upon the external world, who you are has been and always will be pure eternal potential. Anything less is a denial of self and a holding pattern of pain and posturing. Your worth is not based upon something or someone outside of you it is within you. Your moods are ever changing and linked to something outside of you; whereas, your spirit is eternal and unaffected.

Living congruently with who you declare yourself to be is the most honorable and enjoyable way of living. The person with the most certainty of self influences his or her world rather than being influenced. Being a person of influence allows you to transfer positive influence to others; it is a state of being empowered. Now that is an identity worth claiming. Get to know the grandest vision of you, extend an invitation to the best of you magnified from the inside out, and claim worthiness. Here's to You!

Get to Good Identity

An identity for reinventing, reminding and reinforcing an empowered you. *Get to Good* can be used interchangeably with Get to (Empowering Identity) Get to (Name), Get to God, Get to Goddess, Get to Alignment, Get to Empowerment; be playful and be *easy* (as my daughter says) about it.

I AM

Aligned	Allowing highest self to come out and play
High Vibration	A match to my desires
Abundant	All that I am and All that I want
Person of Influence	Creator of my world
Quiet Confidence	Less is more
Integrity	What I want is How I feel
Loved	Well Being naturally
Adored	Of course
Worthy	Allowing the energy in rather than resisting
Intentional	Purposeful
Prosperous	Abundant
Visionary	Connected to highest self always
Playful	Present
Youthful	Expanding wonderment
Beautiful or Handsome	Thank you!
Thought Leader	Birth to new thought offering new desires
Elevated	Transcends reality
Inspired	Spirit in action
Empowered	The power to control my world
Successful	A State of mind not a destination
Joyful	Permission Granted
Appreciation & Self Love	Vibrational Match to Highest Self

The Power of Thought

You are always thinking, what are you thinking about lately? What are you being thoughtful about in your life today? Does it attract or repel your dreams? Be conscious to your thoughts and you can declare the life of your dreams. It is not too late or too early, the time is now. It is no coincidence you are reading these words as they relate to your life, this is a moment of pure potential if you will claim it, allowing the Universe to move in harmony to support you. Simply put *Get to Good* and only good can come to you. Imagine the possibilities.

Being the Universe is an inclusion Universe, it only hears what you say you want whether it is serving you or not. Your thoughts are received on a frequency similar to radio waves, what frequency are you emitting? What program are you tuned into for your life?

Intentional thinking allows you to conspire with the Universe on a conscious scale and frequency. How many times have you thought of something and then is appears? Voila! Whether it is a material object like a car or dress or a person and you notice the car on every road, dress on the cover of magazine or receive a phone call from the person, beyond serendipity, was it or was he there all the time in your existence and you are just now bringing them into your awareness or did your intention create the manifestation? Either way it was by you consciously intending that allowed thought to materialize. How powerful are you that whatever you give intention and attention to will manifest in your life? This is not to be taken lightly, for you are the creator of your life.

The Law of Attraction states that which is like itself will be attracted. If your thought is your invitation what you are you inviting in to your experience? What are you being intentional about in your life? What do you intend to happen today? Is this how you would like your day to unfold? Be clear of your intentions and choose only those that serve you.

We all have access to the greatest infinite resource called our mind; if you choose to master your mind you will command a life worthy of you. Mastering your mind takes commitment, conscious creating and intentional focus. The result of a mastered mind is harmony with the cosmos or simply put getting all you ever truly wanted without compromise. Without mindful intention you end up at the effect of chaos. The power of the mind is not new you have heard it before so I will ask you again how do you need to hear it, see it, and feel it so you will get it now and *Get to Good*?

Be Mindful

Mindfulness is intelligence and love. It is the state of being fully in tune to your highest good and all that is good. Society usually operates from an unconscious state of mind allowing the ego to take over and lead. The ego is the antithesis of mindfulness; it is ignorance and fear. All that being said, is it not exciting to think you now know how to live in alignment rather than ego altered state? The answer is a simple Yes; anything less or more is the ego talking aka sophisticated excuse. Noticing is the most important part; it is when you are conscious to your way of being that you can actually be the person you were intended to be. So if you notice life may not be working for you then alignment is at play and actually working for you are becoming conscious and mindful. Perhaps prior to *Get to Good* you did not notice at all and simply took it as, "This is my Life." Believe me there is so much more waiting for you to create, abundance is circulating in your life right now; allow your intention to be a match to your desires.

Do not confuse being mindful with sitting in lotus pose all day and night or giving up luxuries in your life, being present illuminates life and makes everything vivid and alive. You can be mindful while you commute, work, spend time with your family, by yourself, and live your life. You are not to trade in your western clothing for eastern garments; you are to expand your intelligence knowing alignment in this very moment matters most to you and your world. Giving attention to that which is worthy of you would be synonymous with *Get to Good*.

Embody the belief that you are more than your circumstance. If you adopt this one belief and live it as truth it will transform your life forever. This is not to be taken lightly for who you declare yourself to be is not contingent upon anyone or anything else. You were born for greatness; allow your life to reflect your pure potential. You may be going through a challenging time in your life right now, where you feel you are being tested, stressed and questioned, perhaps viewing the situation as hopeless, a failure, lost cause and it may be that under this pressure and upset you have become fearful, depressed, not yourself lately and I will say to you *Get to Good*. Claim the power for yourself rather than giving it to the current predicament or circumstance in your life. You are not your problems or your triumphs; you are not your designer clothes, your car, your bank account, your career, your partner, your socio economic status, family, social circle or significant latte. Who you are is not based upon what you do or what you have, who you are is everything that the human eye cannot see; all that is invisible yet visible and ever present. It is your Higher Self. Who you have been and who you always will be is found when you *Get to Good*.

It is when you amplify your potential that you become mindful. Being mindful or conscious is being love. Although you might consider yourself learned and intelligent your thinking and actions can be ignorant. Ignorance is driven by fear, it may show its ugly face through jealousy, competition, dishonesty, greed, and living below potential; it is all the same for it is the absence of love. In every moment we have a choice: fear or love, ignorance or mindfulness, choose wisely. Who would you rather be the person who knows how to read and reads or the person who knows how to read and does not read? We know the latter one is acting ignorant and I know you are not ignorant. ***Ignorance is to ignore your potential.***

Intentional living is putting emphasis upon your desires. Being conscious to your life allows you to notice the illusions or delusions you may have created in your life. It is not until you are mindful that you can actually use it to serve. If you live in a state of "Life is an Illusion" at least create it the way you truly want it by being causative and mindful.

The meaning you attach to your life determines your level of joy and fulfillment. What meaning have you been giving your life events lately? Last night, this morning, and your world? What if you attached new meaning to it, added a positive spin and magnified the good and shrunk the bad, would you feel and think differently about your life today? Does the meaning have to be all pervasive and dramatic in your life? Notice the meaning you have been assigning to daily events and check in with this query: Does my thinking elevate or disintegrate my world? Sometimes not making a life event mean anything, allowing you to let go, may actually mean everything. Do you see your life through the eyes of a creator or realist? Many of you have a warped interpretation of life limiting you from experiencing life the way you truly want it. You will always get what you truly want and you will always get what you truly do not want; it is all a matter of focus and intent.

Elevated thinking begins within. A conditioned thought is a belief. Either your beliefs serve you or limit you from accessing your potential. One bad thought does not make for a bad life. Be mindful rather than monitor for thinking more good thoughts than not. You already possess all the power within it is simply a matter of you recognizing it and utilizing it so it serves you. Your world within creates your outer world or world without, all beginning with being conscious to your thinking and emotions. This affords you to be in tune to your vibration for guiding you on creating the life you really want; otherwise known as intentional living.

Law of Cause and Effect

Vibrations supersede manifestations. Thoughts and emotions (feelings) are the source for all that is a reflection in your life today. Your life today is a direct result of causative actions from yesterday, last year or even a moment ago. This moment is the residual of prior moments and the projection of the future. Simply put, the law of cause and effect states that every effect must have an adequate cause that existed before the effect. Every human thought is a Cause that sets off a wave of energy throughout the Universe creating desirable or undesirable effects. Actions produce consequence, which can be perceived as either good or bad.

If we were to take a look at your life today we might speculate upon what you were thinking over the course of your life. It is your thoughts and feelings that produce results. The result is in proportion to the intensity of the feeling and the format of the thought. It is a simple equation Good Thoughts + Good Feelings = Good Results or Less than Good Thoughts + Less than Good Feelings = Less than Good Results. There is no in between, thoughts and feelings fall under one of two categories: good or less than good. The focus and choice is yours by being conscious to when you think and feel good and continue or when you think and feel bad PAUSE and shift your attention to good. Remember it matters not how you *Get to Good* so long as you give attention to only that which does feel good. *Get to Good* Lifestyle Conditioning will offer tools and processes for accessing good anywhere anytime with anyone.

Remember most of you may have the sequential order reversed; you look at your effect or result and then decide how to react and who to be. Reverse it; for it begins with you in mind, being mindful to the power you have in this moment to affect the next. Think of what you want five years from now, tomorrow, this evening, this moment and choose appropriate thoughts and feelings to create, attract and manifest the result you want. It is only when you claim your power in this moment that you can affect change. Transformation in life exists in this moment, what you do with it is up to you. Are you coming from a place of internal power or relying on the external power to determine your destiny? And if it is your internal dialogue, allow it only to serve you, elevate you, and empower you to be aligned with your all pervasive identity. Too often we allow our minds to take us on a journey of disillusionment, distraction and worry or the ego in disguise. The ego cannot survive in a state of being mindful for now is everything the ego is not and this is a good thing. Being mindful is having full access to your potential and desires. The ego is disguised in your own voice so it can be confusing and distracting, probably the very reason when you want to be present you can easily find a number of things to allure you off this moment, this is ego undercover.

The Law of Cause and Effect in your life today: what does your bank account reflect about your thinking and feeling, your love life, your body, your career, your purpose in life? Does your net worth have a lot of commas or is it closer to zero? Net worth is equal to Self Worth; what have you been thinking about your worthiness to create abundance in your life? Do you have a Hero or Zero in your life? Is your body a temple or a tomb? Is your career your calling or a means to an end? Is your life filled with inspiration or obligation, effortless living or stressed existence, clarity or chaos? Knowing where you are in life allows you to fine tune contrast into expanded desires for intentional living. It is then that you have a choice to elevate your thinking or not for you believe, think and feel something all the time; be mindful. What have you been thinking to produce the results in your life today? Are you Ok with it? Would you like more of what you truly want, expanding your potential and creating infinite possibilities? You cannot continue to observe contrast and get what you want. You have an inherent desire to evolve, there is nothing you can do about the past except to forgive and extract the wisdom so you can positively influence your future with intentional living. Please focus your energy on what it is you want to create rather than what you should have done, missed out on or regret. Whichever thinking you choose will only bring about more of the same, the latter unconscious thinking will only keep you stuck in perpetual loss and pain. If you want more from your life expect more from you. You will live into your expectations, what are you expecting, expect good and anticipate something good is going to happen.

Priceless is the ability to control your mind and thoughts. Your net worth is not your material possessions; it is your ability to use your intrinsic power (the power of your mind, body and soul) to deliberately intend that which you really want for you and your life. Power is combining focused thought with intent. Access Universal power for the power that lies within you is far greater than anything manmade or made up.

So how does one define success in life? *Success can be defined as your ability to feel good anywhere anytime with anyone.* When you become clear that all the tangibles and intangibles you have created in your life are the effect of your feelings, you will begin to focus only on how you feel. Feel good and expect good results; feel bad and expect bad results. When you are mindful you are in tune with feeling good otherwise you go to default thinking. Your infinite intelligence or intuition communicates to you through feelings. Feelings communicate in a much more powerful way than any other language, listening to your feelings is the difference between getting what you want and living by default. Feelings are the fuel to creating your desires into reality. Remember we are not going to relate on your feeling bad and prolong more of good gone bad; rather we are going to speak of feelings that inspire and empower you to be the man or woman you know you are beyond circumstance.

What is it that you are looking to accomplish in life? To discover, achieve, possess? Is it really a material object or tangible result, something you can put your arms around and physically touch or is it the feeling you think it will give you once you have it? Think of all your desires, what is the deeper desired feeling you are anticipating once desires are realized? Consider the desire to be financially free, what are the feelings you are looking for: certainty, peace, abundance, security, success, and happiness. The desire for a loving relationship, what are the feelings you are looking for: adored, loved, joyful, sensual, safe haven, comfort, nurtured. The desire for health and fitness, what are the feelings: energy, vitality, youthfulness, sexy, strong, and flexible. If all you desired did not have the added benefit of evoking positive feelings you may not be so excited about achieving your dreams. What good is being married to the man of your dreams if you do not get to feel good while being married, driving the latest model luxury car if you do not get to feel good while driving it, being healthy and fit if you only feel pain? So we can come to the conclusion that what you want in life goes beyond the object, event, or person, it is the feeling or emotion you will have once you achieve it. So if these are feelings you want who is to say you cannot identify those desired feelings and feel them right now?

Does the material item really have to be present to feel the desired feelings; do you really have to wait *until* before you can access good feelings? If you wait until the evidence of your desire shows up you will be a match to more waiting rather than your desire. Allow me to remind you that all of these good feelings you long for are already circulating in your life right now whether you have experienced them before or expect to do so in the future, they are available to you this very moment. An all access pass to feel good now has your name on it. Every positive feeling you long for is present, simply by the mantra *Get to Good*. And once you allow yourself to feel good now you emit a positive frequency into the Universe calling to you more good feelings. The good feelings become perpetual in your life, a successful way of living. High vibration and frequency living is not contingent upon the external world it relies solely on the internal I AM! Where you may get confused and in the way of having a good life now is you think an action which causes an event is the way to feel good rather than feel good being the first causative action leading to inspired action causing good results. The Universe is responding to your consistent thoughts of feeling good rather than your determined actions.

The world is a mirror reflecting back to you your internal energy, psyche, and beliefs, so whatever you project onto the external world (people, events, experiences) will be reflected back to you, similar to a boomerang effect. Life reflects back to you what you inherently possess, the wisdom you need to move beyond a life lesson and the opportunity to show up mindful. The Universe will provide in accordance to your thinking, she does not discriminate, edit or exclude. By Law it simply is so. It is a matter of projection; you project onto others and the world a bit of yourself whether positive or negative. The external world will reflect back to you your strengths and areas of improvement. If you continue to think scarce thoughts you will continue to look for scarce evidence disguised in reality like bills, unfulfilling relationships, or feeling sick and tired both mentally and physically. When you are upset with someone else and get hung up on what they did, you need to check in with what you are projecting onto the world. If you find yourself doing this often then it is time you found something purposeful to do with your time. If I become too curious and overbearing into my husband's daily agenda he clearly lets me know I need to find something productive to do and it does not include him **Oh My Stars.**

Your upsets really have nothing to do with the person, it is only your internal unrest projecting onto another so you can see it manifest in front of your eyes. Perhaps reread that one more time. Significant others, parents and children are instrumental in being our mirrors for our potential and calling you to be more. Certainly not always convenient but definitely worthy of you if you are willing to look internal rather than make it about someone else. Simply saying Thank you for the reminder is a good start. I am an advocate for believing and seeing one's potential even when they do not believe, I would prefer this from others as well. Consider the alternative, not being called to be more is really saying I do not believe in you and your potential, yes stay there stuck in your small story for it is all you can handle in this lifetime . . . *nonsense.* No thank you, not for my readers. It is important to note that you will always have a feeling of being out of control and powerless if you expect another to define who you are going to be in any moment. Just as your projections are all yours, you can know the same is true for others projecting themselves onto you. It has nothing to do with you, do not make it personal, think leave me out of it or not my drama. It is your response to others where the power resides. Once you begin to own your world and the feedback you receive from others and the Universe you can begin to create a life you have only dreamed otherwise known as The Good Life. Everyone you know is off the hook of you being powerful and you are off the hook of another's empowerment. I applaud you for being powerful.

While many of you might not want to own the responsibility of the negative people and experiences that occur in your life, it was an origination of your thought. And then there are those who say I own the majority of it but sometimes life just happens it is a matter of chance and luck; it does not have anything to do with me. I would challenge you to look deeper and notice the correlation between the event and interaction that occurred and a deeper intention you may have been thinking for your life. How were you feeling, were you saying the words but not feeling the connection with your heart and soul? Is this person or event in your life to bring wisdom and deeper understanding? If you allow the experience to be rather than resist or tolerate you will get the lesson and evolve to new levels otherwise you can expect the lesson to repeat itself until you get it.

Elevate your mind and allow your potential to come out and play so you can experience the good life. The answers you seek come from alignment. *Get to Good* anyway you can and often so it becomes A Mantra for Life. Complemented by *Get to God!* **It becomes you!**

AH! THE GOOD LIFE

The Promise of *Get to Good A Mantra for Life* will be a co creative process, the paradigm shifts in thinking and lifestyle conditioning rituals listed in the book complemented by implementation and integration according to you. The intention of *Get to Good* Lifestyle Conditioning is ***personal alignment as a lifestyle.*** This will allow you to access your potential anywhere anytime with anyone. A belief is a conditioned thought. Conditioning just like practice will allow you to fine tune and finesse the *Get to Good* rituals for accessing alignment at will. Remember "What you practice in private you will be rewarded for in public" conditioning is your private time. Think of it like an active meditation emitting a positive frequency for more to come into your experience, the majority of the "work" if you will is done during conditioning then you can move effortlessly throughout your day being mindful of *Get to Good.* Just like water and breath, alignment will become a way of being for you.

Conditioning complemented by intention and consistency allows you to embody and envision *Get to Good.* The Universe is responding to your consistent thoughts and feelings of abundance not haphazard invitations. You are welcome to read through all of the *Get to Good* Lifestyle Conditioning first and then choose a ritual to be mindful for ten days for proper time with conditioning. It is recommended that you begin with Good Morning Me and Good Evening Me Conditioning and go ahead and include them as a standing order in your day. Think of it like your daily vitamin with a 100% recommended dose of Natural Well Being.

Listen, if all you did the rest of your life was call upon the mantra *Get to Good* throughout your day you would shift and see the evidence of it expand. Being called to read this book I can only presume you are ready and willing for more hence *Get to Good* conditioning for the thought leaders and enlightened ones of the world.

A Bonus: All conditioning can be applied to all areas of your life and to those who are in your life; *Get to Good* lifestyle conditioning can be implemented for you and your well being, spirituality, parenting, relationships, prosperity, career and the world. By you embodying an empowering identity of one who chooses *Get to Good* you will grant others permission to do so as well. You cannot control others it is simply you being you and your response to others where you power resides. Take this time for yourself and empower your world. Thank you for being You!

Good Morning Me and Good Evening Me Conditioning

#1 Recommended as Ongoing Daily Lifestyle

Good Morning Me 10 Sacred AM Minutes

Ten Sacred Active Minutes devoted to you every morning, a time for the expression of your infinite intelligence and highest self. This is not rote routine; rituals are intended to transcend you. This is time scheduled in advance, not let us see how the day unfolds and then I will fit alignment in my agenda, it is setting the tone for your day for allowing good. If you think you do not have the time then you are right or if you think I will create the time then you will prosper. Take the time to line up your energy and action will become irrelevant. Think Align then Act.

It is an active meditation or mindfulness for conditioning in vibrational beliefs complementing your desires, mastering feeling good in your body and rewiring for abundance.

Using the time for intentional moments devoted to you and your life, full concentration is given to the abundant you! It is the space and time where you will focus with deliberate intention upon who you are and what you want in life; only focusing on what it is you want to create and attract. This is your life intention and creation conditioning exercise, granting permission for all that you want at an accelerated pace. We always get what we truly want, allow Good Morning Me to be the daily practice to ensure you are attracting only what you truly want. A day well lived begins with you. Providence will move to support one who is committed, expect greatness.

Good Evening Me 10 Sacred PM Minutes

Ten Sacred Quiet Minutes devoted to you every evening for reflecting, redirecting and dreaming. This is a quiet meditation for writing in a journal, meditating, and using your imagination to serve you. Good Evening Me offers you the privilege of asking Who was I today? Giving attention to a day in the life of you. As a bonus, it sets the tone for a night of rejuvenation and energy alignment while you sleep waking up refreshed for The Good Life tomorrow.

Rituals for Active and Quiet Mindful Moments for Alignment:

Declare Vibrational Beliefs out loud
Declare *Get to Good* Identity I AM _____
Get in Nature
Go for a Walk
Journal
Listen & Dance to Music
Yoga
Meditation or Sit Quietly
Exercise
Have Fun & Be Playful
Look for ways of being in your daily life that you will deliberately intend upon during Good Morning Me
Creative Play with Art, Sculpting, Writing
Take a Bubble Bath
Vision Board
Spa
Ask empowering questions throughout your day
Notice when you feel good and call upon it at will

It matters not what you do it matters what you are thinking and feeling while you are doing. Ten minutes of alignment is not in direct proportion to ten minutes of the good life, think of it as an exponential emission of good. Mindful that you are being the creator of you, your experience and life so that it is a pure reflection of your Highest Self and Highest Vision. The purpose behind Good Morning Me and Good Evening Me is to fill you up with the good stuff, not add to your To Do list, it is to remind and inspire you of your greatness, get grounded and peaceful with who you are and tap into an unshakeable mindset of infinite potential. It is not to be taken lightly. This dedicated time is your private time so you will be rewarded during private and public time. Rewarded with feelings of peace and quiet confidence as you go forth in this world, rewarded by living a life from an aligned identity influenced by you internally, rewarded with effortless harmonious prosperity and abundance, rewarded for being a person of influence, and rewarded for living into your vision. Ah . . . The Good Life!

Most of society is running around chasing the clock and their dreams; allow Good Morning Me and Good Evening Me to be your guarantee for manifesting your dreams. It is the difference between someone who believes life has highs and lows, ebb and flow, good and bad, winners and losers, those who truly get it and those who get by and you who does not fall prey to small thinking and feeling powerless. Think of it as your perfume "au de alignment" or pleasure pill. Make no mistake I know who you are now *Get to Good* and get on with the good life.

Go ahead and exhale . . . for there is no right way to engage in your private moments, it will evolve and resonate for you with experience and creativity, the key is to engage it, make it a part of your daily experience like breath and water. Enjoy alignment for the pure sake of alignment and watch your world transform. Accessing the feeling of alignment before the evidence of abundance shows up is priceless and then do you know what? The evidence will show up. When you command high expectations from yourself the Universe aligns with you offering elevated experiences in return. This is the act of being in integrity with the Universe. You will be rewarded to the level you are playing so you may as well play big on this planet. It is no coincidence for the one who is living the good life; looked upon by others with admiration and inspiration "I want that" is practicing *Get to Good* Rituals. Without it expect uncertainty and chaos, with it expect to get what you want. Intentional alignment is the greatest gift you can offer yourself and in return others. Enjoy being you!

Speak Powerfully

Get conscious to living from a source of inspiration rather than obligation. The words "Should and Suppose to" are a couple of the lowest vibration words translated into any language. When you find yourself saying "I should" or "I am Suppose to", what you are really saying is it would be nice I would like it but I will not do it, do not count me in, it will not happen for me, no thanks, and I will pass. It is cousin to the buzz identity procrastinator as if declaring to the world that you are a procrastinator gives you permission to live less than your potential and for what prolonged pain? Should is a weak stance, it is similar to try which I recommend you replace with willing. When you say I am trying you are giving your power to the external world, when you say I am willing you are the cause in your life. Get conscious to your internal and spoken dialogue. Replace *should* with *I intend* and replace *try* with *I am willing* . . . watch the transformation move from postponement to creation.

Beyond semantics, speaking powerfully reinforces a powerful message to your subconscious as well as commands attention and influence by others calling good into your experience. Speaking powerfully says *I believe in me* and *I can access my potential at will.*

Get to Good Language

Find replacements for tentative language: Kind of, maybe, we will see, sort of, perhaps, I do not know.
Replace Should with I Intend or I Choose

Replace Try with I am Willing or I Commit
If you happen to say these words, no worries, simply restate your thought powerfully.

The person with the most certainty will influence the conversation. Speak powerfully and clearly so you can lead thought in the direction of your desires serving all who have the privilege to be in your sphere of influence. When I was visiting an Ashram in India a sign read *"Silence is the voice of God"* less truly is more.

Ownership

Ownership needs few words. Transformation cannot take place until ownership is present. I Am, I Do, I Will, I Can. Be Mindful of "Less is More." Speak in first person "I" rather than third person "You or They" for commanding your subconscious for accessing your internal power.

The most important dialogue you will have all day is that with yourself. Remember alignment is the relationship between you and your higher self; allow your conversations to be empowering, uplifting and abundant. A tall order one worthy of you.

Meaning and Perception

Notice the meaning or perception you attach to your life experiences, daily interactions and your world in general. Sometimes making something not mean anything means everything. A recommended replacement word for what you might have considered intense meaning in the past is to say Hmmm INTERESTING! I use this all the time. It lightens the load allowing for you to *Get to Good* much more quickly then if you use a few chose phrases that cannot be included in the book. Play with this and have fun noticing how you feel better by using INTERESTING rather than explicates charged with negative meaning. The meaning we attach to something or someone determines our level of joy in the moment; hence Alignment. Notice Universals as well like: always, never, every time, every one and all. Use Universals only if they serve you My life ALWAYS works out for me rather than I ALWAYS get the short end of the stick. Give meaningful attention only to that which is worthy of you otherwise it is interesting but certainly not all consuming.

Get to Good **Shift Words** *empowering alternatives*
Interesting
Oh My Stars!
Indeed
Nonsense
WOW
A Smidge
Oh Well
Of Course
Is that so? So what! What is Next?
Get out of your own way, get off it and *Get to Good.*

Identity Ritual

Recreating & Embracing the Grandest Vision of You
Implement the Identity Ritual in your Good Morning Me for
the next 10 days:

"I am who I will to be" Charles Haanel

A. Capture a list (unedited version) of all the qualities you love,
possess, and would like to exude. If you think of qualities you
do not want focus upon what you do want, sometimes it is
the antithesis. Think of people you admire, real or imagined,
whether you know them personally or not and add their qualities
to the list. This list is for your eyes only and it is ongoing and
evolving. You already possess all the positive qualities; it may
be that attention needs to be given so they become magnified.
As you review your list, access your senses on how each of
the qualities would feel in your body, how you would move,
what you would say, what would you believe, and the tonality
of your voice. What thoughts would enter your mind, what
decisions would you make, how would you see your world?
Amplify your talents. Visualize it and own it now.

Hint: Add all the *Get to Good* Identity Qualities listed in *Good
on You*

Choose an Archetype or symbol which best represents you and
the qualities you have chosen. It is a one or two word identity
that reflects an all-pervasive identity for you. For example
A Goddess, Diva, Gentle Giant, Platinum Princess, Hero,
Money Magnet, Rhino, Orchid, Ferrari, Diamond, Greek
God, Superstar . . . whether mythological, natural or made up

it is your choice. And you will know it is the identity for you when it resonates, when you say yes this is WHO I AM!

A. Condition in your new identity over the next 10 days in Good Morning Me. Declaring out loud while in motion with your body whether by walking, running, dancing, yoga or deep breathing: Exclaiming I AM Empowering Identity, then I AM Qualities saying the qualities you listed for yourself.

B. Strategically place top of the mind reminders of your new empowering identity, reminders are to access all the senses: Consciousness, Smell, Sight, Sound, Taste and Touch they can be pictures, photos, material objects, quotes, colors, textures or scent. Ideas for placement of mindful reminders: screen savor, refrigerator, key chain, night stand, car, office, home, dash board, shower, diary or agenda, mindful of accessing your identity anywhere anytime with anyone. Good Morning Me allows the identity to evolve from your Higher Self while the mindful reminders are triggers to your subconscious. You cannot have too many *Get to Good* reminders.

C. Ask Empowering Questions throughout your day
Am I Showing up as Empowering Identity?
Does this Serve Me?

Congratulations on discovering and recreating your new empowering identity. You are timeless; you have always been and always will be the highest intention for good, be mindful for living a life of alignment from an empowered identity. Enjoy the evolving of you and the life you are creating, do this for you. Do you need others to recognize your empowering identity or can you simply BE? Allow the world to be moved by the introduction of you.

Shortcut to Your Desires

Allow Feeling Good Now and Creating The Good Life

1. Think of your desires you have for your life having already been achieved, actually living the life of your Dreams.
2. Feel all the emotions you experience by living The Good Life.
3. Capture your desires, wants and The Good Life feelings in a Journal
4. Begin to feel those emotions NOW
5. Notice how feeling good positively transforms your day
6. Condition and practice feeling good even if feeling less than good enters *Get to Good.*
7. Experience consciously creating the good life by the power of your thoughts and feelings; the vibration you are emitting.

NOW VIBRATION	FUTURE DESIRE
Feel Good	Aligned
Loved & Adored	Life Partner
Abundant	Financial Freedom
Purpose & Passion	Calling
Joy & Harmony	Fulfilling Relationships
Vitality & Appreciation	Health
Elevated & Enthusiastic	Successful Career
Empowered	Making a Difference

You say you have desires but how do you feel about your desires? In order to bring about your desires you must become a vibrational match (feelings and thoughts) to your desires.

Vibrational Match Beliefs

A belief is a conditioned thought! What vibrational beliefs would you want to embody to be a match to your desires?

Declare 10 Vibrational Beliefs for conditioning in Good Morning Me

Discover your passion and purpose in life

Do something creative every week even if you have never done it before or think you are any good at it or have not done it in a long time. Get the creative buzz flowing to bring attention to your passion and purpose in life: Art, Dance, Sing, Extreme Sport, Exercise class, College Course, Vision Board . . . Creative Activity

What do you Love? Schedule 2 things you love this month in your agenda.

The Story of Your Life

1. What do you want in your personal and professional life?
2. What is your story or spin about why you do not have it yet?
3. Think beyond what is so, what could be your new story and spin on life?
4. How will you feel once you achieve what you want?
5. What decisions will you make to support your big story?
6. Feel the desired emotions, what inspired actions will you commit to scheduling in your agenda to achieve your desires?
7. Celebrate being a person of potential!
8. Begin to tell The Success Story of your life. Be Bold!

Zen Cleaning

I know you have heard it said before, "Less is More" a paradox worth understanding how it applies to your life; less low energy thoughts allows for bigger thinking, less worrying allows for creative dreaming, less clutter allows for clarity, less of the bad allows room for the good. But if you hoard the bad there is not room for the good. You choose what you want to occupy your mind: positive, high energy good thoughts or negative low energy not so good thoughts. Rather than letting go think allowing good.

Your external world is a reflection of your internal world. Look around your home, office, car and notice if it is clean, organized and a reflection of your highest self or is it cluttered, disorganized and little resemblance of your highest self? I could walk into your home, look at your attire and the way you care for your clothes and appearance (beyond the cost of attire), visit your office, ride in your car and know what must be going on in your head and heart. And you thought you have been doing such a good job in covering up the chaos in your mind. Well you have just been found out and be glad for it, now you can be compelled to do something about it. I know you have reasons for your desk looking the way it does, a big project; clothes appearing as an afterthought, a new dry cleaner or housekeeper or your new fashion look; your house, waiting for Spring cleaning . . . and so let us be clear that your spin on the *why it is less than the reflection of your grandest self* will only keep you from receiving all the abundance and prosperity that is waiting for you.

Zen Cleaning Strategy

1. Do I like it and will I use it over the next 12 months?
2. Does it reflect my new identity?
3. Do I need it or will it benefit someone else greater?
4. Is it time to sell it, give it away, or recycle?

Hint: You may need a Zen Accountability Buddy to help you in this process of letting go and you can return the favor. Keep in mind: if you hold on to the old you will have less room for the now. This applies to energy, thoughts, space, things, and experiences. A sacred space that is a reflection of your pure potential magnifies and attracts more of the same.

Zen Cleaning is a foundation for creating a sacred space externally aligned with your longing to be clear internally. Space fills for time and room allotted; allow it to be a reflection of you. Vastu is an Indian philosophy of harmonizing space through mental clarity leading to physical clarity. Implementing Zen Cleaning allows abundance, big thinking, and clarity the space it deserves to enter your world. Zen Cleaning is the process of taking stock of everything externally in your life; homes, cars, offices and other spaces you control and clearing out making room for the good in your life. Sometimes we even have to look at people in our life and decide if a relationship needs redefining allowing for harmony and fulfillment.

Get to Good Nano Shifts

Discover ways to feel good anywhere anytime with anyone. You are the only one who knows what feels good to you beyond words. Nano Shifts give you the advantage of accessing good in the moment. Many of you have mastered feeling stress now it is time to give concentration to that which is worthy of you, mastery of feeling good.

Nano Shift Implementations

Ask Empowering Questions	Redirect your thought
Deep Abdominal Breathing	Connected to Energy Center
Posture elongated and grounded	Open up Meridians and Align Body
Sip on Water	Body and Brain made mostly of H2O: Hydrate
Look for evidence of good in the moment	I get whatever I focus upon
Whisper a belief to yourself	Aligned communication
Sing your favorite song	*Get to Good* Lifestyle Conditioning
Move your body	motion creates emotions and vice versa

Mindful reminders on key chain, computer screen, desk, refrigerator, pocket, wallet, handbag and mobile phone Discover your personal *Get to Good* Shifts

A State of Appreciation vs. Gratitude

While gratitude is a wonderful quality more times than not it comes with an afterthought of lack. I am so grateful I have a _____ because I do not want _____. While contrast can be good for gaining clarity upon what you want it is important to direct your thoughts toward that of abundance rather than the afterthought of lack.

Beyond semantics, it is a comparison of desires to contrast of what you no longer or never would want, call it what you will, for sake of clarity it will be referenced as gratitude.

Appreciation is noticing and embracing an abundant mindset and vibration without the lack afterthought. It is a Polaroid snapshot of all that you love and all that is minus the comparison. You are simply taking mental photos of Yes I like that and that and Oh that and then you allow it to expand, similar to the financial phenomenon compounding interest. Appreciation is giving proper attention to your interest and anticipating it will multiply.

Appreciation is the quickest way to get into Alignment or *Get to Good*. Practice looking for evidence of good in your life, day and this moment; you will find it and more importantly you will get to know Alignment.

Abundance is circulating in your life. Look for and expect to find evidence of good in your life.
What do I love in my life?
Who do I love in my life?
Who loves me?

What is good in my life?
What do I have to look forward to today?
What feels good right now?

Today I will look for only that which I want to see and I will find it.

Touch and Go: Get off less than good and *Get to Good!*

The Power of Thought complemented by Questions

Questions direct your focus. You are continuously asking questions from the time you awake until you fall asleep; some serve you while others are disempowering.

The Art of Empowering Questions

ALIGNMENT Do I feel good? Yes or No Answer; if Yes get to know it and magnify it if No look for evidence of good, What would feel good right now?

WHO Am I showing up aligned and abundant?
WHAT do I want?
WHY do I want it? (Purpose behind your desires)
INSPIRED ACTION (Elevated How rather than self imposed limiting how) Effortless living is taking action from a place of inspiration rather than obligation, it is when you take the time to line up your energy first then move with inspired action. You will be amazed at the level of fulfillment and accomplishment you will experience today without losing self or feeling overwhelmed. Be a thought leader and see beyond *what is* using visualization and imagination. Inspiration transcends how.

Why does this always happen to me, why not me? Presupposes there is something wrong or missing with you. Why is best utilized for discovering your purpose and passion for your desires not to question self. Self inquiry always self doubt never.

How and Why questions can be misleading and scarcity driven. How will I accomplish my dreams? Immediate roadblocks will show up disguised as reality and logic.

End every thought with an Elevated Thought!

While contrast can offer clarity on what you do not want or no longer want in your life; practice ending every thought with an elevated aligned thought. Let the stage you are launching from be that of Alignment and Abundance.

Jacqueline ISMS

OH! My Stars!

Get to Good!

Less is More

Leave the party when you are having fun

What you practice in private you will be rewarded for in public

One person who is aligned is more powerful than one billion who are not

The person with the most certainty influences the conversation

Be the person God intended you to be

Worry is the misuse of your mind and talent

High Vibration

Magnify your potential not your problems

I Am (insert your name) and All is Well

A Call to Be More

It Becomes You

Permission Granted

Elevate your mind

The Universe will meet you at your desires may as well dream big.

Give attention only to that which is worthy of you

Of Course

How can I be a match to my desires? What will I conjure up today? Who will I collaborate with today? Am I showing up aligned? Does this serve me?

You are more than your circumstance

Allow your potential to come out and play

My Pleasure

A Tall Order

Nothing needs to be wrong for a transformation to exist

Patience Grasshopper
You never need to justify your existence
All desires come from alignment
Alignment transcends logic
To be the man or woman God intended you to be

Jacquelinelnternational.com

Please accept my personal invitation to become a member of VIP Coaching!

Visit me www.jacquelinecornaby.com

CPSIA information can be obtained at www.ICGtesting.com
Printed in the USA
LVOW06s0414050614

388623LV00002B/2/P